What Readers Are Saying about
A Spiritual Friendship

"Never has a conversation touched my heart and soul more. I love it, and recommend it to anyone interested in building their own spiritual friendship."
– Chuck Cochrane, Co-author of *Heart and Soul Resumes*

"These letters reveal lives dynamically lived in a contemplative way. Enjoyable, informative – a real pleasure to spend time with these two."
– Rich Heffern, Associate Editor, *Praying Magazine*

"A treasure, a precious pearl. Thank you for the gift."
– Maure Quilter, M.A., M.F.C., Lafayette, California

"This book exudes warmth, friendship, love, and a very special sharing… (and its) loveliest thing is encouragement…the idea of a spiritual friendship is very appealing, very nurturing."
– J. Buskirk, McIntosh, Florida

"I found so many points that were just for me right now. People interested in spirituality would love a course on this book."
– Betty Gaiss, O.P., M.A., Educator, Lansing, Michigan

"The perfect guide for anyone who desires to blend spiritual principles into their everyday lives."
– Donna Peerce, co-author of *Heart and Soul Internet Job Search*

"This book made me more aware of the spiritual connection between my sister and me… We really are spiritual friends more deeply than I had realized."
– Betty Crawford, The Sea Ranch, California

"An inspiring written conversation between spiritual companions that encourages us to focus on ideas and resources that we need to grow toward our best lives."
– Dee Roshong, Ph.D., Dean, Counseling and Student Services, Las Positas College

"These letters provide insight into the process of becoming true to one's self – the essence of a true vocational path."
– Christine Otis Skinner, Ed.D., Career Counselor and Director, Carleton College Career Center

ANONYMOUS

A SPIRITUAL FRIENDSHIP

...and while they are yet speaking,
I will hear." – Isaiah 65:24

WomanWell
1784 La Crosse Avenue
St. Paul, Minnesota 55119-4808

A Crossroad Book
The Crossroad Publishing Company
New York

The Crossroad Publishing Company
370 Lexington Avenue
New York, NY 10017

Copyright 1999 by Anonymous c/o The Crossroad Publishing Company

All rights reserved. No part of this book may be reproduced, stored in a retrieval system, or transmitted, in any form or by any means, electronic, mechanical, photocopying, recording, or otherwise, without the written permission of the Crossroad Publishing Company.

Printed in the United States of America

Library of Congress Cataloging-in-Publication Data

A spiritual friendship / (the editors of Teleios Center).
    p. cm.
  Includes bibliographical references and index.
  ISBN 0-8245-1765-2 (pbk.)
    1. Women mystics — Correspondence. 2. Poor Clares — Correspondence.
  3. Mystics — Correspondence. 4. Spiritual Life — Christianity.
  I. Teleios Center
BV5095.A1S65   1998
248.2'2'0922--dc21
  [B]   98-20666
                                                                         CIP

1 2 3 4 5 6 7 8 9 10   04 03 02 01 00 99

*In honor of the
sweet significance of a
spiritual friendship,
the Teleios editors dedicate the
following collection of letters to
Sister MF
and her spiritual companions—
The Abbess and the Sisters
of the Monastery of St. Clare—
and acknowledge the fruitful years
they have spent together.*

TABLE OF CONTENTS

EDITORS' FOREWORD
(An Animating, Elemental Wisdom) ix

January: A Reoriented Life 1
February: A Hidden Preparation 15
March-April: On Fruitful Relationships 24
May-June: High Synergy and Peace 33
July: A Self-Emptying Turn of Mind 39
August: Toward a Universal Sanctity 47
September: Improved Effectiveness 61
October: A Spirit of Oneness 67
November: More Mary Than Martha 87
December: Vital Daily Life 97
January: Summing Up 107

EDITORS' AFTERWORD
(Conversations at the Vital Ground of Being) 121

NOTES 123

BIBLIOGRAPHY 127

ABBREVIATED SUBJECT INDEX 129

EDITORS' FOREWORD

An Animating, Elemental Wisdom

If a mother loves and nourishes her daughter according to the flesh, how much more must not each one love and nourish her sister according to the Spirit?
— SAINT CLARE

SPIRITUAL FRIENDSHIPS are only informally religious. The hallmark of a spiritual friendship is its tendency to encourage devotional authenticity, and it bears witness to the Divine companionship. By definition, a spiritual friendship animates the elemental wisdom or heart of each individual involved.

This brief volume chronicles the maturing of a long-distance friendship between two individuals. Each comes from a different walk of life. One is a cloistered Catholic nun. She spends her days within the confines of a gated, religious community. The other, an author, lives a self-styled contemplative life. The former, a Poor Clare Sister, has taken vows to uphold the Rule of her Order. This includes living contemplatively in community with her spiritual companions. The latter is a Christian mystic who, characteristically, finds her fulfillment in a reflective solitude. Each finds evidence of the Divine everywhere.

The two friends share a deeply reverential sense of Oneness. For them, that oneness with God is a progressive, experiential certainty, not a theory. Their modes of being are marked by simple, joyful recollection in Christ. Despite the superficial differences of their lives, each is a contemplative. This means, paraphrasing Thomas Merton, being (a) one who takes God seriously (rather than taking some "means" to God

Foreword

too seriously); (b) being famished for truth; and (c) seeking to live in simplicity, in the Spirit. An ardent and sincere humility is the best furtherance for this solitary life that relies on God and not technique:

> *The contemplative way is, in fact, not a way. Christ alone is the way, and he is invisible. The "desert" of contemplation is simply a metaphor to explain the state of emptiness which we experience when we have left all ways, forgotten ourselves and taken the invisible Christ as our way.*[1]

The evolution of the friendship

We begin to know the two friends as they got to know each other: slowly, politely, affectionately. By the time we meet them, the two have already settled into a loosely-knit routine of monthly exchanges.

Through a year's worth of letters (and transcribed audio tapes) we journey — meditatively one would hope — into an evolving relationship, one built on a trusting exchange of religious experience born of solitude and contemplative commitment.

Without a fussy piety, the friends unfold their devotional perspective. Their correspondence is at once open, yet somehow closed — edited to omit the most private disclosures while preserving that degree of intimacy readers require to savor the substantive underpinnings of an ongoing spiritual dialogue. Repeatedly one gets the sense that the issues of personality, self-improvement and routine social chit-chat are irrelevant to a spiritual friendship. The companion, as Abhishiktananda — a French monk and writer who lived in India — once noted, is

> *God, or more precisely, God in the mystery of the Incarnation of Jesus Christ, the unique Lord, who comes to meet me under the form of this or that human brother or sister ... In this person it is God who comes to me, requiring of me that, through my respect and love, through any humble service that I may possibly perform, I should help this*

Foreword

person to draw out of himself the potential for divine life which is hidden in the depth of his spirit.[2]

The two have asked to remain anonymous. This suits their purposes: The completion and full flowering of faith, sincere love of and mystical union with God — not psychological, intellectual or even personal exposition. We learn more through the letters of that hiddenness as a mark (especially of the mystic type). Many personal asides are included in the letters but these feel more like the flavoring of a *self*-vanishing, individuated soul. St. Bernard proposed there were three distinct vocations in the monastic life: "...that of Lazarus, the penitent; that of Martha, the active and devoted servant of the monastic household; and that of Mary, the contemplative."[3] Mary is called to live and worship in a meditative fashion, and this is the "best part," but not always understood or even desired by others.

The first letters reveal the background of each friend's life. Their concerns seem similar to ours with one exception: Most of us struggle to achieve balance *in* the world, but these two aim to *dis*entangle themselves from it. Like Mary, they sidestep family, social and work relationships that encroach on their spiritual loyalties and focus their daily contributions on their highest goal: Lasting union with God. In other words, Oneness.

Format and organization

Each group of monthly letters opens with a short editorial overview about spiritual friendship — what it is and isn't, and we read about upcoming themes. Wherever appropriate, a few words are included about the mystic's way and contemplative spirituality, two topics the friends repeatedly consider. Every reasonable attempt has been made to track down and cite the references of the friends' numerous informal quotes. Some comments in the letters refer to taped or personal remarks that have been omitted and are best understood by the overall context of the conversation.

Readers will note that a spiritual friendship is marked by an

Foreword

absence of spiritual direction while it encourages the sincere living out of God's Word in daily life. The persistent unfolding of practical wisdom within each friend's "living out" and articulation of her faith originally sparked the letter-writing process. Over time we note that "each one loves and nourishes her sister according to the Spirit."

Their self-and-social transcendence, their affinity for prayer and contemplation, their appreciation of little natural events and creatures, and their overall love of Scripture may lead *us* away from the world's patterns of attainment and toward Light. In sum, as they cross their Jordan to take possession of the good land which is their inheritance, spiritual companions turn their minds increasingly toward that incorruptible and greater life, for their God is a consuming fire.[4]

The *Teleios* Editors

A Spiritual Friendship

January
A REORIENTED LIFE

ST. CLARE *(Clare di Favarone) has been called the most faithful follower of St. Francis of Assisi. Francis himself installed Clare and her spiritual companions in the "run-down little convent of San Damiano"* [5] *where they put down their own religious roots. Here, Clare discovered her life's purpose and developed a "marvelous synthesis" of the original Franciscan spirit of devotion, with its "concentrated spiritual activity of the strictly cloistered life."* [6] *This life continues today, as we now read of it through Sister MF's remarks.*

January's exchange opens with Sister MF's lengthy response to H's Christmas gift — a slender memoir. Numerous personal asides introduce us to each friend's life, her likes, dislikes and inclinations. Both began their professional lives as teachers, and each renounced certain creaturely comforts (i.e., a familiar way, the understanding circle of family and friends, selected securities) for a spiritual existence.

Sister MF's initial missive casts light on the desolation each felt in letting go: As she empathizes with her friend's move to a wilder-

ness, MF injects elements of her own story into her letters, and we see she, too, felt compelled to affirm an inner call without precisely understanding why.

In fact, the dissonance felt between what is and what could be precedes all spiritual growth. Dissatisfaction with the material world is a typical dynamic of contemplatives who, ultimately, reorient themselves to solitude or cloistered living. Certainly this reorientation is true of mystics [7] who respond vividly to their deepest inflowing of intuitive wisdom. Unlike most of us, Christian mystics ascribe not logical but supernatural causes to their summons, as did Meister Eckhart who saw the spiritual connection in that interior prompting and cautioned us not to question the call:

> As truly as the Father in his simple nature gives his Son birth naturally, so truly does he give him birth in the most inward part of the spirit, and that is the inner world. Here God's ground is my ground, and my ground is God's ground. Here I live from what is my own, as God lives from what is his own ... It is from this inner ground that you should perform all your works without asking, 'Why?' [8]

January

January 1996
(Transcribed Tape)

Shalom, H.
Today, Friday, gives me a hunk of time to respond to your memoir. It is tremendous — a gift to your friends and to anyone who reads it.

So I will begin with brief reflections, although I'm not sure how brief they'll end up being. It was wonderful that you used a quote from the C. S. Lewis' *Voyage of the "Dawn Treader."* How beautiful. To break our enchantment, we must sail to the world's end: You repeat that line a few times, which I loved. I see your life like that — it's opening up and you are being that explorer. *On breaking enchantments*

Your introduction made me realize that you wrote this book for those who have encouraged you and for those whom you encouraged. Reading let me learn some things I didn't know but somehow suspected. For instance, I felt that you'd been married and were probably divorced. I couldn't see how anyone as bright and attractive would not have someone who loved her. Then, as I read about the people you loved whom you didn't include in interviews (your grandmother, your mother-in-law, your neighbor and friend, GJ), I discovered how many close, dear friends you've had.

Many of those interviewed described you as "playful" and said you have "applied good humor." You don't know that side of me, but I dearly love people with a playful temperament. They bring out mine. Sometimes my humor is corny (I love jokes and get hokey with the sisters, so they tell me.) All those who are dear to me have those qualities: Easy good humor, virtue and certainly compassion. *On good humor*

In your chapter about your days in education: I loved your stories of the children. You handled them so kindly when they were naughty. Your friend, J, sounds wonderful to be around. I appreciated her observations that your colleagues wondered about you: "What do we do with this person who is so different, who wants to do new things in new ways, instead of in the same old manner?" I resonate with that. That was my tendency, too, as a teacher. When I came here, I learned to be more subdued. Being more contemplative, I'm coming around now, yet still innovative in my way — without causing everybody around me to be upset. That's my challenge.

On the genuine interest of others

I have marked enjoyable pages. For instance, one on which you write,

> Genuine interest from attractive, attentive strangers is an antidote that nourishes pride of self and a performance so necessary to healthy morale.

Maybe I've taken a liking to you, as the saying goes, because you saw good in me, and you were a basic stranger. Originally, that lifted my morale. Just before your memoir came, I was looking around for something to read, to get settled in during the January-February syndrome — that dreary, after-Christmas mood where one must get back up and going again. When your book arrived, it gave me a spark. I hadn't felt like writing or thinking or doing anything. Just hibernating — and hibernating at the heart, too. So your point about "genuine interest" fits there.

Here in this life, as I've noted before, what we really need is genuine interest: To give it and to receive it. Frequently we keep a lot of things to ourselves, and then these issues come out sideways. When we hold meetings with all the Sisters and Brother E facilitates, he lets us ventilate. He's a psychologist with good humor who helps us laugh at ourselves.

On healing choices

You wrote, "*The progression toward healing choices resides at the heart of person-centered psychology, and certainly healing choices are the soul of good health.*" Often Sister M and I say when we have a choice to make: We can do something "not so good" or we can make an "elegant choice." We owe that language to the book *Elegant Choices, Healing Choices*. We knew that before, of course, but that work clarified the concept.

I enjoyed your saying that when you felt someone was unkind, you learned to say, "Ouch. That hurts." The ability to express those hurts isn't easy, and I must learn to do more of that. And Rilke's truth that human beings strive to remain uniquely themselves at all cost is absolutely accurate. I definitely agree that feeling safe in the world is "the greatest instinct of our unconscious." I also like this point:

January

Every change-agent needs at least one trusted friend to talk to regularly, and not just during troubled times. Sadly many leaders routinely shoulder every heartache, confidence and organizational burden alone.

I wish every Abbess had that luxury because that leadership reality is very true for them.

I related to your admission that, when all was said and done — agonizing or not — you just "shoved off" toward new ventures, despite the fact that pulling away was a painful self-surgery that demanded all your resolve. That you left teaching, that each old separation-trauma from your past required healing before you could leave and that your mending process took years (and even therapy) to attend to conscious grieving for hurts sustained in early life taught me something new about you. In your life you must have really made some healing choices. One of your neighbors describes your good friendship with your former husband and says that he now lives not far from you. It's easy to imagine the pain you must have experienced with all that loss.

Leaving all things

I, too, left teaching to come here. I'd been a Sister of Charity in Ohio, where my sister still lives (and is a Sister of Charity) and had wanted to do that for so long and finally did it, but leaving that life was wrenching. I also taught in Denver, which I loved, what with its mountain peaks and wide-open, spacious scenery. All these images are still in my mind, so I really understand what your leaving teaching and your home must have meant, maybe even more for you in the sense that you had so much to give up. It's like when the Apostle Peter says in the gospels, "We have left all things to follow you," and what did he have? A few smelly nets. Maybe a fishing boat. That's all he had, I guess. But you had much to give up.

That letting go is trust, an invisible wave of Love permeating the very nature of people and things. Love is sufficient to transform, or elevate, a beneficent self-awareness, and Love moves us toward our life's plan. Even chance remarks radiate that love. When I was considering coming here, a Sister of St. Joseph's said to me, "How will you know unless you try?" That did it. That, and another Sister telling me she was going

Letting go as love

A Spiritual Friendship

to Africa because, as she said, "I've always wanted to do it." And I thought if I *don't* do it, if I don't enter a contemplative order now, I probably never will.

Chance remarks as love

Another chance remark, which perhaps you'll enjoy: Before I decided to move here, I was standing in line at a Burger King. At that time I was not wearing a habit and was standing with several other Sisters. One of my friends sneezed, so I said, "Bless you." And a three- or four-year-old — no more than that — looked up at me and said, "*God* bless you." I'll never forget that. Now I always say, "God bless you." A three-year-old taught me that. Chance remarks can change your life.

On separations and wanting to quit

When I was in Denver on retreat, the priest who said the Mass seemed to be waiting for me when I came out of the chapel and said, "Oh, I hear you're going to the Poor Clare Monastery." Then he added that he had first joined the Trappists but left. He said, "You'll frequently feel like leaving, but don't. It's worth it all." To this day I don't know that priest's name but thank him so often for saying that. There were times when I've wanted to leave. The transition from an active teaching job to this contemplative life was not easy, but I remember his words repeatedly. He mentored me and brought hope with that brief insight. That's what I find in you: Such optimism. It's wonderful. It's what I really like.

Encouragers as mirrors

You say from a Judeo-Christian perspective, we might view our reliable encouragers as outer reflections, mirrors if you will, of some vital life force already in ourselves. St. Clare uses that image of the mirror, too. I find that link so interesting. We are told that "mirror literature" was popular among the religious of the 12th and early 13th century.

St. Clare and mirror literature

St. Clare added significantly to that line of thought by developing its Christological and feminine qualities. She writes in one piece (referring to Christ) that that mirror was suspended on the wood of the cross. Later on, she tells us to be that reflection for others: "*We should be mirrors for those who must serve as mirrors for others.*" She wrote many inspired letters to St. Agnes of Prague (who was actually a princess, a daughter of the King of Bohemia) who left all things to become a Poor Clare. In one letter St. Clare wrote,

January

Gaze upon that mirror each day, oh, Queen and spouse of Jesus Christ, and continually study your face within it so that you may adorn yourself within and without with beautiful robes.

Then before she died, she told her Sisters in her testament,

For the Lord himself has placed us not only as a form for others in being an example and mirror, but even for our own sisters whom the Lord has called to our way of life as well. Since the Lord has called us to such great things that those who are to be a mirror, an example to others, may be reflected in us.

Others see themselves in us and copy themselves after us. We become mentors for them, and then they become mentors for others as well. In our Franciscan study, we're told a great deal about this, so that analogy meant a great deal to me.

On social and self-transcendence

I've read about traits like self and social transcendence as lifting one's consciousness above egotistic and cultural certainties. Sinetar, the writer, calls that awareness "a 21st Century mind." Some people illustrate that. I believe John Paul II is much like that, already thinking of the 21st century.

I related to your saying that from grade school through grad school, through early professional life you'd been scolded for forwarding too many novel ideas. You upset the status quo. I've experienced that, too. That's why I write poetry (what I call "musings" — I don't know if it's poetry). It's a creative outlet, my own way of expressing things. And I write letters of social conscience to everyone, from the President of the United States to Saddam Hussein. These are my ways of preserving my innovative spirit.

As you say, tranquility puts things into perspective, strengthens focus and self-renewal. As I get older I realize that when I am not at peace, I'm not focused and forget things. Inner stillness requires us to wake up early to pray or meditate before work. I get up early to pray so that I can focus on the day. I really need quiet time. Amen to Hasidic scholar Martin Buber's suggestion that only in the stillness does our soul burst through the commotion or noise of everyday life.

A Spiritual Friendship

Inner stillness

After reading your thought that stillness asks us to stop chasing after praise or excitement and settle into the commotionless joy that is life, I read St. Frances de Sales' instruction:

> *Do not wish to be anything but what you are and try to be that perfectly.*

It was a coincidence that I happened on those words while I was considering "commotionless joy."

Learning to say "no" and learning to live more simply and quietly reminds me of Henry Thoreau's *Walden*. That book helped me choose to come here. Thoreau wanted to see if he could live simply. He only did it for three years. That same aspiration brought me here, looking for a place where I could live simply.

Crosscurrents

You write that Thomas Merton longed to be shut up in a hermitage and do nothing more than be in direct contact or intimate union, with God. But another part of him was forever dreaming up plans and projects. That is us, isn't it? Thomas Merton went to Asia. I took my trip to Assisi, Italy, and to Poland. You admit to having one impulse that enjoys being embroiled in all sorts of projects and another that moves you toward a quiet, worshipful life. Our temperaments must be similar.

Personal asides

When he did my evaluation thing, Father S said that I was the sort of person who would keep learning my whole life — into my 90s. He added that I needed time for contemplation, to be away from everything. He said that need, too, will be lifelong. You seem that way, too. Sister M said that you are just so creative. Neither of us means that in the sense of praising you, though that's there, but merely as an observation and truth: "Innovative, creative and highly intelligent" is what we called you. I like what J said about you: "She's contemplative, not at all social and has zero interest in gossip or political debates." I relate to that, too, not liking gossip at all. I also enjoyed P's comment that your attention centers us in our *own* thinking: That the source of your animation and energy is the Holy Spirit.

Energy and the Holy Spirit

You write that when the Holy Spirit acts in, or through,

January

even one person, everyone within that person's sphere gets blessed, becomes energized and loving, if only for a time. Here again, I'm reminded of St. Clare, one of the first women to ever write a Rule, who advised her Sisters that even the youngest person in the community should be fully heard; the Holy Spirit's action showers compassion on all:

> *Let her consult with all her sisters there concerning whatever pertains to the welfare and good of the monastery for the Lord frequently reveals what is best to the least among us.*

In the text is a note that "the least" is sometimes the youngest. However, Clare substitutes "the least" for Benedict's "youngest," thus underscoring the gospel teaching found in Matthew 11:25-30:

> *Jesus said, "I thank thee O Father, Lord of heaven and earth, because thou hast hid these things from the wise and prudent, and hast revealed them unto babes."*

Another point you made which I liked was that:

> *One generous selfless gesture is enough to spark a cascading of good, since love never fails.*

Linked to that notion is my tendency to give up what I want to do, for the good of the community, and to do what I want if it doesn't hurt the community. That's a selfless standard I've learned to live with. If something is going to bother the community, then I "give." *On selflessness*

You say I come across to you as humble. As Thomas Merton said, "Humility looks good on somebody else." (You know, "I'm humble and proud of it." I hope I'm not that sort.) *On humility*

I'm glad that you're able to speak of your spiritual life to me. Such dialogue generally sparks the soul's own song of life.

C's wonderful insight about the unfolding of talent appealed to me, especially his saying that it is "like trying to find the edge of the ball, one edge makes up the next edge, which makes it the next, and so on." The spiritual life is like that, too. Saint Therese wanted to be a ball in the hands of *Spiritual life like a ball* the Lord, to let him toss her wherever he wanted. Often we think the spiritual life is like a stepladder that we climb in linear fashion, from purgation to the illuminative, to the unitive way. But I love this idea of a ball: Finding its edge makes up our next move, and so on in an eternal progression. That's a beautiful concept.

Growth and learning as spontaneous

You stress that we must stay ever open to the adventure of locating life's overarching themes and interests and that we flourish as a result of extending these interests and our friendship to others and that others do not "improve" because of us. I never, never thought of that.

I imagined, you know, that we become better because of others or they become better because of something in us. I never considered that we need not get puffed up with pride due to our efforts, or that people grow because growth and learning are spontaneous to life.

On Fundamental Goodness

It seems, for you, imperfect people, "plain by worldly standards, shine with fundamental goodness and the light of supernatural love." This reminds me of Thomas Merton who, when he visited a shopping mall near his Trappist monastery, said he felt totally overcome with the goodness of the shoppers there. When he first went into the monastery, he felt he was leaving the world because it was bad. Later, he saw the goodness of people — in their smiles, in the courtesy of a grocery store clerk. I see that, too, when I go out. Ultimately, people are so good that I am just overwhelmed. When we all go out, some ask, "Why does everybody talk to you?" Probably because I smile and talk to people. The Abbess teases me when I go out to buy something. She says, "They'll offer it to you as a gift or will beg you to take it." Sometimes that happens, but I never look for it. I suppose because I'm present to the clerks no matter how ordinary they are, that changes lives for the better: Simply being fully present liberates some healing energy.

Strength derived inwardly

Returning to that young man, C: I especially admired his statement that you have "an absolute bull's eye on how people work, how they're motivated ... There's an unspoken energy involved in this." He says being with you is like being with a calm, highly-focused monk: "You sense that this person has

January

something going on inside. I'm not sure where monks get their strength, but I imagine it's in part from the way they live." That's so true. Monks do exude peace because of the type of persons they are. And by the way they live.

A friend of mine, RB, is a lawyer and lives nearby. We took Hebrew lessons together here at the monastery with a larger group. Rabbi T taught us. Ours was a wonderful class — quite diverse. Neither RB nor Rabbi T seemed to mind my being blunt. We're open to discuss ideas, and no one took offense. We just engaged in an exploration. RB always says if there are 12 Jewish people in a room, there will be 13 opinions. I like that: Not debating, not arguing, just throwing ideas out and being forthright, while trusting you're still accepted.

Another point that struck a bell for me is when you speak about how everything in life is holy. The Jewish tradition offers us a prayer that can be said after one's morning bath. It praises the synchrony of our organs and is said in gratitude for the gift of our body. From a book Rabbi M gave me:

On timeless prayers

> *Praised are you, Lord, our God, king of the universe, who with wisdom fashioned the human body, creating openings, arteries, glands, and organs, marvelous in structure, intricate in design, should but one of them by being blocked or opened fail to function, it would be impossible to exist. Praised are you, Lord, healer of all flesh who sustains our bodies in wondrous ways.*

That's really beautiful, isn't it? I love the prayers of the Jewish people. Christianity is rooted in them, and these timeless prayers bring us back to the Jewish Jesus, to his Semitic lines. I'll just add that when I've wanted to learn something about Jesus, I've called Rabbi T for information. Once I said, "I'd like to know more about the Semitic mind." He cracked up and asked, "What is that?" He laughed so hard that I explained, "Well, I feel that if I know the Semitic mind, I will better understand Jesus as well as our gospels." He answered in turn that he's always wanted to say to all his Christian friends: "You've got to comprehend Jewish thought before you can understand your Jesus." You would love him. Rabbi T has

A Spiritual Friendship

a comeback for everything. One time he said that, in the Jewish tradition, it's unheard of not to get married. The person who does not marry is blemished in some way. I said, "Well, Jesus did not marry," and he replied, "Ah, but Jesus would have made an excellent husband." He is also so witty, so playful.

The core self: a gift of grace

Your whole last page is just lovely where you write that the Spirit of Truth has guided you, that truth alone has power and that the encourager lives in anything or anyone who helps you search out truth in the hidden wisdoms of your heart.

So that's what I think about your wonderful book. I'm sending it to Bishop Charron who will be enthralled with it. I just feel a special link with him too, and in a sense you encourage me to send this by what you have written.

Now I will let you go.

MF.

January

January 31, 1996

Dear MF,

Thank you so much for your thoughtful tape, notes and feedback on the memoir. How satisfying to hear you enjoyed it. The others interviewed had similarly gratifying reactions. My heart is full. The two years spent on it somehow invested the project with more meaning and brought more satisfaction than I can express.

The experience brings me to the realization that when we receive "thirty, sixty or a hundred fold" from what we give, that's true giving. Certainly true giving is above and beyond mere material exchange. Further, certain *arenas* or types of giving may be more ours than others. (Like Mother Teresa said, "You can do something I can't do — I can do something you can't do ...") I heard recently about a woman who, when someone complimented any item of hers, *forced* herself to give it away. Is forced giving true giving? A legalistic following-of-rules or an indiscriminate showering of materialistic, obligatory attention seems oddly less blessed than when we're moved out of Love's compassion to give in a *particular* direction. It is more blessed to give than receive, and yearning to give signals real generosity is present and at hand. How generously Jesus gave to us ...

True giving

I mailed out the last of the memoirs last week after a normal day of calls, writing and work. I was bone tired. My office was damp and freezing. I was hungry, and my head hurt. I determined to keep going so as not to make anyone wait any longer than necessary for their book. The *instant* I committed myself to press through my fatigue and complete the task, a wave of gladness uplifted me, and I felt, "Ah, this is *real* living — this moment of full engagement, or heart giving, is the highest joy one can have." Given that you've devoted your entire life to such giving, you are much more aware than I am about that experience.

I want you to know how grateful I am for your tapes and correspondences and will write a longer letter when I have more time. Here is another copy of the memoir for you to

Personal asides

give away. Now you can keep two for yourself and have the rest to do with as you choose.

You sound well and happy. I am, too. I don't know exactly what to do with my hermitage project. If I center all my attention on it, I can build it as a nonprofit and make it quite grand and impressive. Yet something within says, "Stop." There's a catch or hold in my spirit. A huge part of me wants only to write, to live quietly and encourage others from an unobtrusive place. This vision still hides. Do pray that I "catch" God's idea and promptly express it. I'm often slow to get the message.

All peace,

H.

February
A HIDDEN PREPARATION

*T*HE MYSTIC *perceives everything as an agent of sacred transmutation. Along these lines, despite brevity, the February letters tell us of the mystic mentality and of a contemplative's intent to love one's neighbor as self.*

H sends photographs of her home in a remote rural area and describes the synchronous events leading to its purchases, underscoring earlier remarks about the mystic's way. There are believed to be three universal elements to the mystic way:

- *Purgation (wherein one leaves all else behind for That Which summons),*
- *Illumination (the sense of supernatural Good in everyday life as, by grace, one perceives God dwelling in one's own soul),*
- *Union with God (the mystic progresses in love, a path that culminates in a "new infusion of vitality" as the old self merges with its divine source, or as Aquinas said, "The last perfection to supervene upon a thing is its becoming the cause of other things."[9])*

A Spiritual Friendship

For the mystic, the whole world works in unison to enflesh the body of that interior experience—until the fullness of spiritual expression is brought out of the mists.

In turn, Sister MF gives us a glimpse of the Franciscan (and therefore St. Clare's) stance toward others. We are told St. Francis began every greeting with a right intention and a poetry of heart that loves the other as self. Sister MF's short quote reveals that posture as her own mind — the sentiments that call her imagination toward the sacred are befitting of Francis' love for commonplace creatures and the glorious alike, as he said:

> *All creatures have the same source as we have. Like us they derive the life of thought, love and will from the Creator. Not to hurt our humble brethren is our first duty to them; but to stop there is a complete misapprehension of the intentions of Providence. We have a higher mission. God wishes that we should succor them whenever they require it.*[10]

February

February 3, 1996

Dear MF:

I listened to more of your fine tape while driving to the market today and laughed when I heard your picture of my evenings. True, I often do build a fire. But, I relax by watching television: the Simpsons (a hilarious, off-color cartoon series); if possible PBS — *Fawlty Towers*; a mystery (Miss Marple is my favorite heroine) — A&E's biography series. Or just junk.

Enclosed are some pictures, one of which — the photo of Jung's home — illustrates a divine synchrony. A decade ago, before purchasing my home here in the forest, I endured a long, fearful decision-making process. (Later I realized God unfolds us in total harmony. We need make no big "decision.") Anyhow, having just left the public sector the prior year, I wasn't at all established as a writer. This rural location is a 15-hour drive from my old home down south, so I'd drive up Friday afternoon and return on Sunday night — after hounding local realtors to help me find a small, aesthetic house. I had an exact idea of what I wanted, but what I saw and could afford were diametrically opposed.

On divine synchrony

One day a friend phoned to say, "I found your home!" No one wanted it, and it was off the market. As we drove down the winding driveway, sunlight streamed through the mist and redwoods pretty much as in the photo. Instantly I thought, "Well, I can see myself living here." Even the interior held promise, although at the time it was dark and overly rustic. The price was high. I told the realtor, "I'll think about it" and chugged home, worrying all during the drive about things like financial risks and mortgage payments.

Back home, in the mail, the enclosed postcard of Jung's home in Switzerland greeted me. The card had no return address or signature but was imprinted with Jung's motto: *Without my piece of ground, my life's work would never have begun.* (I've always wondered if he meant by that not just the physical soil, but also his "ground of being.") The next day I purchased this house and have lived here ever since. What was worthless to others was invaluable for me. *"Show me,"* said

The foundation stone

17

A Spiritual Friendship

Jesus, *"the foundation that the builders rejected, and that shall be the cornerstone."* Neat, huh? Not a single day passes without my being thankful for the grace that helped me move. And now I want to move still deeper into the wilderness.

I'm traveling for research purposes so won't write for a while. All peace in Christ,

H.

February

February 12, 1996
5:45 a.m.

Dear H,

Peace and all good. (By the way, that phrase *Peace and all good* is what St. Francis said before he began to converse with people. Francis also prayed all night with the mantra, *My God and my all*. Beautiful.)

Thank you for your letter and the pictures. In Jung's book *Memories, Dreams*, he mentions wanting a tower as part of his house in order to be more spiritually centered. Interesting that your home looks so similar to his in style and forest feel.

We have a new priest from the Divine Word community where Father P lives. The new priest, Father M, is from Poland. He's studying at a local hospital. In his thirties, he's a breath of fresh air for us. His liturgies are just wonderful (as are Father P's). He has a wonderful sense of humor. Even his eyes sparkle. *Personal asides*

When I told him my mother was Polish and that her maiden name was M_____ski, he said, "Oh, royalty! It is beneath you to speak to me — a peasant." He told me (and I've heard it before) that if a Polish name ends in "ski" it is from the old nobility.

Well, enough for now. More soon. Father P said he loves your memoir and is sharing it with my spiritual director.

Much love and shalom,

MF.

A Spiritual Friendship

February, 1996

Dear H,

More on hiddenness

An afterthought from St. Francis (related to something you said on the phone about liking a certain hiddenness): From one of his biographers comes the word that Francis was cautious about revealing what he called "God's secrets." Once he asked his brother friars what he should do, for instance, should he admit freely what he had seen in a vision?

The brothers advised him to be more open and forthcoming. They said that when God reveals his secrets to us, it is not for us alone but meant for others, too.

In other words, the consensus was if he hid something intended for the good of others, then he was burying the talents that God gave him. But Francis thought otherwise. He replied, "It is for me to keep my secret to myself." Then he convinced the other friars that God had revealed some things to Francis he never would tell anyone, as long as he lived. [11]

I thought this dovetailed with your sense of it "not yet being your time" to reveal your own spiritual vision.

On devotional bibles

Also, I am sending a running commentary devotional by Oswald Chambers, who, while not a Catholic, has given us all one little meditation for each day. I had seen his *My Utmost for His Highest* advertised and told my friend about it, and she said, "Oh, you don't want that. That sounds so devotional, so pious."

Then, while reading *America Magazine*, I found an interview by Father George Anderson SJ with *the* Mr. Gallop (of Gallop Polls, from Princeton). Gallop is most interested in religious trends today. When asked, "What do you read?" he replied that he reads *My Utmost for His Highest* and said the book changed his life. And I thought, "Oh, dear."

I found a special, $2.95 edition and thought, "I can't go wrong with that" and asked if I could send for it. When I received it, I liked it very much. Chambers, a missionary, is not pious. He was born in 1874 and died in 1917, in Cairo. When he died, his associates sent a cable to his friends in Great Britain (though he was born in Scotland) that said, "Oswald is in His presence." Isn't that beautiful? I really like that.

February

I take the readings slowly and enjoy them by not forcing myself along. I do like his commentaries.

When I'm reading that bible, I'm thinking of you. In one part, Chambers says there's so much religious gab today. (And he was referring to the period of 1910 to 1914 — now this is a man who died in 1917.) Then, speaking to God he says,

All confidence in God (not things)

> *Have I any confidence or have I got beyond all confidence in myself and in men and women of God, in books and prayers and ecstacies? And is my confidence placed now in God himself, not in his blessings?*

Then he says,

> *I am the almighty God ... the Father, Mother, God. The one thing for which we are all being disciplined is to know that God is real.*

He's speaking of God as Father and Mother, and that's today's conversation, right? Anyway, I wanted to share that with you.

Shalom,

MF.

A Spiritual Friendship

February 1996

Dear MF,

On hiddenness
I feel greatly encouraged by your St. Francis anecdote on hiddenness — the preference of all true mystics, no? (You know, St. Gregory's idea — that we live a heavenly life only by somehow forfeiting the world, or at least, as Merton explains it, by arriving at a balance that fulfills our own unique vocation within God's plan.) Pastor Benny Hinn — a televangelist who's a surprisingly decent scriptural teacher — suggests that the original meaning of *hidden* includes *preparedness* (i.e., we hide while being readied to be the servant and friend of God). Neat information, no? (Job says, "There is a path which no fowl knoweth ... and the thing that is hid bringeth forth to light." [12])

Practicing love
On a recent tape you wondered why, after so many decades of reading Scripture and reflecting on it and living with the idea of Christly love, we rarely *practice* compassion with those we love most or live with. I empathize. Could it be that intense spiritual growth seems to aggravate the human interpersonal sphere? Human ties weaken, even as Love intensifies. We are drinking new wine while pouring out the old, learning to interpret the world anew — from God's viewpoint, not our own. Nothing one humanly does seems of any value.

No self-effort, no psychological analysis, no academic rule irons out those tensions. Only God's grace helps — just relaxing into God. And we learn to rest in God that way when our paltry human attempts to do something decent prove futile, yes?

Here again, the saints inform us, like St. Teresa who said that both solitude and socializing are tortures for the soul undergoing such times, and that the thing is inexpressible for the discord cannot be fully articulated.[13]

That's one value of a spiritual friendship: God loves our working together in ways that glorify Creation, ultimate Reality — as Isaiah wrote:

> They shall not labour in vain, nor bring forth for trouble; for they are the seed of the blessed of the Lord, and their offspring with them ...

February

And it shall come to pass, that before they call, I will answer, and while they are yet speaking, I will hear..[14]

How lovely to rest in these thoughts of God, which after all are totally unlike our thoughts. A wonderful contemporary writer, John Hargreaves, remarks on one of his tapes, "How I love to consort with God's thoughts about me." [15] Beautiful, yes?

Resting in God's thoughts

Paul deJaegher writes along much the same lines, although he comes from a totally different lineage of faith, which only goes to show that spiritual wisdom is universal. The whole world understands the power of Love, whether demonstrated by a Gandhi or a Mother Teresa or some ordinary guy down the street. We all know goodness when we see it — no matter the creed. As you rightly point out, our challenge is to live our theory — to put it into practice.

All peace,

H.

March–April
ON FRUITFUL RELATIONSHIPS

*M*ARCH AND APRIL's *conversation is largely about family and friends. How do we honor father and mother despite our parent's failings? What does it mean to be a true friend or accept others despite our failings?*

All authentic dialogue plants a thought-seed, waters it over time and brings it to fruition only with serious, added consideration. So, too, in letter-writing, the progressive blossoming of ideas comes with thoughtful self-inquiry and time.

Moreover, according to an old story, that wisdom is furthered as we gaze upon whatever illustrates the good we seek. As a desert father said,

> If a hard-working monk lives in a place where there are no other hard-working monks, he cannot make progress: He can only struggle so as not to get worse. But if a lazy monk dwells with hard-working monks, he makes progress if he is vigilant and if he does not get any worse. [16]

In discussing fruitful relationships, the friends focus on the "hard-working" and the faithful. They strive to apply the highest

March–April

standards (e.g., the examples and sayings of the saints and the saintly) to their own comportment, all the while looking their own imperfections straight in the face.

Their remarks add insight into the nature of spiritual resilience — the sort that draws out humility and strength through that poverty that seeks not self-effort, but an application of living love.

A spiritual friend is not a spiritual director. We note in all these letters the near absence of what could be termed "unsolicited advice." Other than recommending an occasional book, each friend scrupulously honors whatever seems like the leading of the Holy Spirit in the other (as well as in herself). Through the mail, each listens actively — and intuitively — to the other, attending carefully to what is and isn't said, reading between the lines to discern and bolster whatever Spirit of grace her friend receives.

Spiritual companions intuitively heed James 4: 4 that,

> *whosoever will be a friend of the world is the enemy of God.*

In other words, each supports the other's hidden heart to encourage the demonstration of God's Word in the practicalities of daily life.

A Spiritual Friendship

March 24, 1996

Dear H,

Peace and every blessing.

Personal asides — Enclosed is a tape sample of my presentation for our Federation meeting in Massachusetts. I used that *Wall Street Journal* quote you mentioned (on one of your tapes) which I liked. I hope to mention some writing of yours that has helped me.

Father P listened to my tape and he liked the content but said to put more life in my voice. He is right of course so I need to practice that.

Your voice has life in it without being aggressive. When I read aloud that quote from the *Wall Street Journal*, if I "hear" your voice in mind, I sound a whole lot better.

Bishop C likes your memoir and is using it for Lenten Meditation.

Brother C from St. Bonaventure University recently told me he has not forgotten about my poetry (*Musings* — a name I like better). He plans to have them printed sometime.

So Woman of God, I hope that you find time to wind down after your travels.

You are held in prayer and may the Risen One visit you in Word, people, events and Nature.

MF.

On true friends — P.S. Another thought on friendship is that our friends accept us "as is." In David Copperfield by Dickens, David tells his friend who was about to run off with a girl David was fond of, "You have no good or bad for me. You are always equally loved."

True friends are that way. They try to love as God loves — a shadow of God's love for us. So, you are easy to feel that way about. Others I may have an aversion to and find hard to accept like that, but I do try to love as God loves each of us — Whee — see how human I am? Thank God for His Mercy.

March–April

P.S.#2 About that friendship, Oswald Chambers writes that our friendship with God is "based on the new life created in us which has no affinity with our old life, but only with the life of God ... absolutely devoted to God." [17]

A Spiritual Friendship

March 26, 1996

Dear MF:

Your voice sounds just fine, as is. In my humble opinion, you don't need to put more life in it (or whatever word that was). Your talk is *most* inspiring. Following the sequence of your remarks was effortless, and your quoted poetry is lovely. So great, good wishes for your presentation. It'll be wonderful and you're bound to leave the platform all enthused yourself. Keep me posted.

On delays

The hermitage project discourages. So many legal and accounting forms for the IRS and hard to communicate an embryonic, ephemeral vision to largely secular advisors. While waiting for the IRS to come through with formal non-profit status, I've rerouted myself to other concerns. In early January they requested further information (promptly sent — by certified mail). Three months have passed. No word. Zippo. Yesterday I phoned again but got no call back. Today I phoned *again*, only to be told the IRS *lost* all the paperwork. They didn't even care. Very matter-of-fact about it. Nearly two years of back and forth mailings, that mountain of paperwork, those grant writers, those committees. (Is this what's called "a sign?") Sorry to unburden myself ...

On honoring mother and father

My new book recounts personal stuff related to my childhood. It's tough to write autobiographically, and for this I need an editor with a good scriptural background. Father M (from Canada) would be my top choice, but he's ill and seemingly needs yet more surgery.

As I write, the scriptural injunction *honor thy parents* returns to mind. I loved both of my parents, and say so — ad nauseam. However, one parent had serious emotional problems (from which I instinctively recoiled). In truth, I'd like to write about that, without casting blame. What's your take on conveying one's "baby truths" without undermining the honor one intends to give parents?

Personal asides

My lecture trip went well. The weather was atrocious: In Washington State it poured and flooded and snowed and iced. Still crowds flocked to my talks. Frankly, I was stunned. Standing room only in one small town bookstore during a

March–April

fierce storm — gales, snow, sleet, and no advance publicity. Some theology professors from other counties (and Canada) phoned personally to apologize for not being there. Others drove great distances, well out of their ways, simply to say, "Thank you." Deeply touching — and simultaneously humbling, and all glory to God for any good that's done. Such experiences give me heart to continue with the new book, with the hermitage. With everything.

You're in my prayers for your speech-making success. Let me know how it goes.

All Peace —

H.

P.S. Your postscript on true friendship is excellent. One of my great flaws is a quick temper with annoying types — no matter who they are. Merton, I read, had his ways of distancing himself from intrusions and people he did not care for. What an inspiration he was.

Thank God we are not expected to be perfect by our *own* efforts. Right?

St. Therese of Lisieux said she was too blemished to compare herself with the saints but concluded nevertheless that "God would not inspire a wish that could not be realized ...." so she devised that small way of loving God "that allowed the imperfect to reach heaven." Sweet, no?

And St. Teresa (of Avila) said she didn't believe we could ever attain perfect love for our neighbor unless we had our roots in the love of God. So there's only one answer: To strengthen love of God. Yes?

A Spiritual Friendship

April 1996

Dear H,

Thanks for your last, long letter. I thought about, and prayed over, your question about how to write about a disturbed parent. Here are some early thoughts:

1) What happens to us when we are young (or old) forms us — everything forms us — so we are products of our formation.

2) If we tell "all" that may ...
   - help us/or others
   - lay guilt on us
   - cause hurt to other family members

3) *The truth sets us free* (or "The truth makes you mad" — an old Persian proverb).

I'll ponder this and write more later.

Also, no need to apologize for unburdening yourself. To me, you come across as real. Thank God. Merton used to say, "I am like the rest of men, thank God." You know the Pharisee in the story of the tax-collector, prays, "I am not like this Tax Collector," and his prayer was not heard. Right?

Shalom,

MF.

P.S. Here is another thought from St. Clare:

God did not destine us to be models and mirrors solely for others, but also for each of our sisters so that they in turn might be models and mirrors to those living in the world.

March–April

April 1996

Dear MF:

Thanks for your card and wonderful quote. I'm swamped right now and know you'll forgive me if I keep this short.

I absolutely *love* the Oswald Chambers book you sent and read a little every morning to set the mind in order for the entire day. Thank you so much.

In turn, please accept these Andrew Murray volumes.[18] I've incorporated both the Chambers and Murray into my morning reading, which now looks something like this: Prayer and meditation; reading of Scripture; the Chambers selection of the day; then Murray. Just a page or paragraph is rich enough to give me something to chew on.

At home in every church

I hope you'll like these. Murray is not Catholic but, like Billy Graham once said about himself, he must have felt at home in every church. I certainly do, and relate to that sense.

I was not surprised to hear that your audience enjoyed your talk and "Musings." (Perhaps just the word poetry, like the word "opera", turns some people off. You're wise to have changed the name.)

Personal asides

In return for the enjoyment received from your last music mailings, here is something different and quite pleasant. The first song, *Amazing Grace*, is sung beautifully. The rest, Country Western mode, I can take or leave. Leave mostly.

An afterthought: I trust you have a CD player?

Anyway, I'm traveling a lot these coming summer months. Some large lectures and ongoing search for that special property I dream about. Not sure just where I'm headed — toward my own aesthetic. And ah — when I'm at home, a rose garden to tend. My favorite.

All gratitude for your steady, uplifting correspondence.

All Peace in Christ,

H.

P.S. Related to your St. Francis quote re: hiddenness is

A Spiritual Friendship

Oswald Chamber's idea that we should leave others alone — particularly vexing types and circumstances — and just ask for Christ-consciousness, and "He will poise you until the completeness is absolute." [19]

May–June
HIGH SYNERGY AND PEACE

Francis of Assisi and Clare, whose quotes we find sprinkled liberally throughout these pages, exhibited a childlike trust in God and a style of thinking that was surprisingly ideology-free.

The letters of Spring suggest the friends are similarly disposed: Disinterested in ideologies, they share a lively, spontaneous enthusiasm for music, for little creatures of nature and for beauty of every sort.

Their informal enjoyments help structure what Abraham Maslow might have called a "high synergy" world-view — a perspective that cultures a benevolent, friendly environment and helps one feel comforted and protected (in the same way that a "low synergy" world-view produces fear, insecurity and constant feelings of vulnerability).

The two are seemingly engulfed by workaday challenges: One dislikes public speaking (by all reports, American's top ranked phobia). The other feels stressed by bureaucratic stalls and mounting paperwork. Yet, in the final analysis, these mundane concerns impose few actual constraints on the friends' good-humored acceptance of life and their own foibles.

A Spiritual Friendship

Each takes herself lightly, while expressing a generous, almost casual spirit toward whatever seems to obstruct her path. Each applauds the other's victory as her own — the latter sense of oneness being another feature of a high synergy relationship, as Maslow explains:

> *... Somehow two people have arranged their relationship in such a fashion that one person's advantage is the other person's advantage, rather than one person's advantage being the other's disadvantage.* [20]

Low synergy friendships, by contrast, are exploitive and conflicts abound around such issues as "who wears the pants in the family or who is the boss." [21]

A spiritual friendship is a high synergy relationship by definition. In Francis', and now Sister MF's words, spiritual friends always wish each other, "Peace and all good."

May–June

May 1996

Dear H,

Thank you for your letter. You never need apologize for shortness or lack of writing. I marvel that you have any time to correspond at all with the amount of activities in your life and am grateful when you do write, wondering what you are up to when you don't, and holding you in prayer all the time.

It is amazing though that when I intend to sit down and write to you, if you have been on my mind, a letter comes from you. It must be telepathy.   *Personal asides*

Thank you for the CD of *Amazing Grace*. Yes, we do have a CD player and the Sisters and I will enjoy this rendition. In St. Anthony's Magazine this month is an article on favorite hymns. *Be Not Afraid* is Number 1 and *Amazing Grace* is Number 2. Some of the Sisters do not like the line, "who saved a wretch like me," but I said (as meekly as I could), "Should we sing, 'Amazing grace — how great thou art, who saved a *pretty nice person like me?*'" Since then no one has commented further, agreeing that the lyrics are more correct as is.   *On Amazing Grace*

I am glad you enjoyed the music mailings.

About my presentation at the Federation meetings: There were so many talks that when I finally did get up to give mine, I felt the audience did not want to hear another word, so that made me nervous. Anyway, I made it through. Some people said they did not notice my nervousness. The Sisters from my house noticed since they know me through and through.

May your new book become a published reality. You have a calling to spread the Word, especially to men. Men need to hear the gentle, articulate spirituality you dispense.

In Peace —

MF.

A Spiritual Friendship

June 1996

Dear MF:

Thanks once more for yet more lovely music. It hit the spot. I am in-between travels, fatigued and unable to do much more than sit around, weed the garden, read and listen to music. I stare at the wall a lot. And out of my window — which looks onto the forest.

On holy nature

I have new neighbors: teeny-weeny tree frogs. They live in the side-yard, right by my bedroom. Tiny, darling creatures they are, glistening green, about the size of my thumb-pad. They've moved into my water fountain (a giant Zen-pot with a bamboo spout from which flows recycled water) and sun themselves on large rocks in that system. What with wee frogs flying about and the hummingbirds (who actually *seat* themselves on the rocks, stick their needle-beaks into the water and drink right out of the spout), my garden shines with pint-sized, iridescent life. Pure joy.

Personal asides

Despite the humdrum travel, summer progresses smoothly. I'm scouting for land for the hermitage project. Next week I fly to Washington state where I've heard of a small, fixer farm house on 40 acres. Probably a shack. Without grants from the now on-hold nonprofit status, a proper house on a large acreage seems premature.

Did I send you the most recent news of how the idiots at IRS lost the hermitage paperwork? That fiasco taught me a lesson: No big organizations for me. I've put the nonprofit aspect of the hermitage on the back burner while moving ahead. I'll find a small cottage, postpone buying the acreage and do all I'd planned minus grants, special tax status or IRS blessings. I don't know "how" I'll do it, but the answer will come when it's ready. Or when I am. Deep inside, in some primal part of mind sits simmering a divine thought, a vision, a directive. And the clear sight to actualize it is at hand. I know it. I've felt this before and it never fails. First Chronicle 17:12 now leads my way:

He shall build for me a house, and I will establish his throne

May–June

forever. I will be his father, and he shall be my son; and I will not take my loving kindness away from him ...*

One interesting aside: Recently, I gave talks at a couple of what might be called progressive churches. One group is two or three generations removed from its founder, with whose work and writings I'm familiar. The minister seems to have no love of scripture, no knack for giving sermons and few intellectual gifts. (Since I'm not mentioning names, I'll divulge this.) Anyway, the parish had zero familiarity with their founder's deeply mystical bent, but in my talk I included a few anecdotes about his peak religious experiences. The audience was spellbound: The scriptural dimension seemed foreign to them. After conducting a short meditation on the Psalms (which seemed to upset some weird, quasi-religious cult group in the audience), again I felt the listeners were enthralled with scripture. (Maybe I only imagined it.)

Impoverished churches

I love the old desert monks and saints precisely because their sayings are so pure — so close to the heart of the gospels and Christ's message. What the world needs now is a few more saints and more innocent love of Scripture.

All best to you,

H.

---

* King James version: no caps.

A Spiritual Friendship

June 21, 1996

Dear H,

Thank you for your nice, newsy letter. Always delighted to hear from you and amazed that you find time to write. After an exhausting meeting, trip or something I just want to be. That you take time to write is appreciated.

Personal asides

Congratulations on winning that award of excellence, per your phone message. It's not boasting to tell of it, merely the truth. And humility is the truth as the Mothers and Fathers of the Desert always said.

I'm glad you liked the music tape. I used it for my retreat and it helped me be less distracted and fussing in the inner chambers of my spirit. I can get so mentally active that I need to quiet down in order to come to a prayer that is centered on the Holy One.

Your new forest neighbors sound sweetly calming to a tired traveler. How wonderful nature is, helping to recreate us each day.

Yes, you sent the nonprofit update about the IRS losing your paperwork for the tax-exempt status. Your quote of 1Chron.17:12 is perfect for building a trusting hope in your venture. (It would be a good one for us, too, since nothing has developed on our plans to sell the monastery land.)

Franciscan peace and justice

The Abbess asked me to be on a committee for a Franciscan approach to Peace and Justice which comes out in workbook form. I'll travel to Boston in September to work on it. In the meantime, my lawyer friend told someone who has a grant to work on "Peoples and Stories" that I might be a good contributor, and the Abbess thought this might add insight for the workbook, since it's a way to work with diverse people, all with different backgrounds. I'll send more details after the first meeting to be held at the Synagogue.

Yes, I heard about that odd group you mentioned when a Catholic psychologist came here to help us with a project. When we found out he was into that cult, that was the end of him. He is now living in California.

Peace and every blessing,

MF.

July
A SELF-EMPTYING TURN OF MIND

*S*T. CLARE *was the first woman to write her own Rule and obtain Papal approbation for it. Her love of poverty may have seemed to emphasize renunciation of material comforts – food, shelter and such – but the point of seeming deprivation was to walk in faith, in absolute trust of the self-emptying that Jesus Christ evidenced.*

That trust depends on refusing to accept the testimony of our senses, resting in God at the heart, and has less to do with the sacrifice of externals, than it does retaining "things" without any real recognition of (or attachment to) possession. This nonattachment was what the rich young man who sought out Jesus for advice on holiness could not manage. Saints on the other hand – whatever their circumstances – have eyes only for God.

St. Bernard was sometimes criticized for traveling everywhere in style. He "expressed great contrition" but said that he never noticed the conditions of his transportation. [22]

So, too, did St. Francis preach to the natural elements – the sun, the moon and stars – and to flowers, in remembrance "of the Eternal sweetness." [23] *He also loved the towns and villages through which he journeyed and lavished prayers on them.*

A Spiritual Friendship

St. Teresa said that looking out at trees, water and flowers took her mind straight to God. Created things may serve as a stumbling block to some, distracting them from contemplative pursuits. Yet even things draw the attention of the wholly spiritual to the Presence of God.

A spiritual friendship illustrates that self-emptying turn of mind. It exists within the context of the most ordinary conditions. Rather than distracting us from our devotions, a spiritual friendship deepens worship by summoning the mind to rest in God.

In this fashion, although the two friends grapple respectively with their contemporary concerns — How to use a computer? How to find a choice piece of real estate at a reasonable price? In sum, how to fulfill normal professional objectives excellently? — they stay focused on God.

Their studies, their sharing of inspirational readings and ongoing dialogue somehow addresses their deepest purpose: To live as transcendent Reality. July's exchanges prove that life is not made spiritual by right circumstances but by habituating that right turn of mind that, no matter what else seems to be happening, is uplifted in God.

July

July 1996

Dear H,

Peace and every blessing.

This letter comes to you hot off a computer which I am just learning to use on my own. There is much that is still Greek to me, but I am getting the hang of it.

We are in retreat. As I am one of the workers at this retreat, I can take time to study this computer, and writing to you came to mind.

Personal asides

We subscribe to that journal you're writing for, and our Abbess handed it to me pointing out that you are their new columnist. Even though that will be an added chore for your already busy schedule, I think they made an excellent choice.

Have you read *The Cloister Walk* by Norris? It is very good. Norris is not Catholic, but is a Benedictine Oblate and has spent long periods at St. John's Abbey praying with the monks. Her love of the psalms, the monastic life and their liturgy impressed me.

Her writing reminds me of yours, except she is more earthy (which I could do without) and also you have something more mystical that resonates with my spirit that Norris does not have, for me.

Yes, the Desert Fathers and Mothers expressed the truth so simply. They had some strong woman writers saying some powerful stuff. A little like your frogs and hummingbirds: Straightout and unadorned.

MF.

P.S. 40 acres in Washington? Splendid. Beautiful nature.

P.S. #2 Thank you for the books by Andrew Murray. This morning I read in his *Prayer's Inner Chamber* chapter 5:

> A man (or woman) in whose heart and life God has taken the right place as the All in All, has only one desire, that he should have that place throughout the world.

Murray's thoughts on the morning watch and how that should/could/would prepare us for the rest of the day made me think again that prayer has to carry over to the rest of the day. As I always say to Sister D., I must watch my words ...

A Spiritual Friendship

July 25, 1996

Dear MF:

Thanks for your good note. Great news that you've got a computer. It makes some writing much easier. (I still edit myself with pen, a different concentration somehow.) I'm tardy in acknowledging some other mail you sent. Writing the column is my least favorite task now — while moving forward with that new book on childhood, possibly my best work to date.

Personal asides

The column is only so-so. Please warn my friends at your monastery, like the Abbess, about its mediocrity and apologize in advance for my faulty writing. First the editors told me they wanted a column on spiritual direction. (A year ago, we agreed I'd address actual questions from readers.) Two months later they said, "Oh, well, we want something from your other work, just excerpt your newest book." *Then* a month later they phoned to say, "Oh no! No excerpts. Write something fresh with lots of practical tips." So now I'm writing my own type of column, rambling and philosophical. The first few were written in mish-mash fashion, what with all the redirection. (The hodge-podge ends about half-way through.) Whew.

By the by, that photo of a retreat house you sent me: Absolutely lovely. Is it in your Diocese? What about that Benedictine order you mentioned? Do they have a retreat house? I'd like a retreat to stay for lengthy periods, by the sea — which is actually where I live now, at home — but completely away from reminders of business. Two monk pen pals hinted that I might make a retreat at the cottage that Merton used (i.e., his Hermitage I suppose). I've stalled on that, wishing so much to be right on the ocean and to hook up with some spiritual direction while there.

In October I'll fly back East to Maine, then back to British Columbia. Not sure yet as my search for that 40 acres is on quasi-hold. I keep my eyes open though ...

On books

I doubt that I'll read the Norris book. It's tough these days to concentrate on contemporary books. I prefer the classics, Scripture mainly. I do like Hargreaves whom I've mentioned

July

and the enclosed by Father Jean Sulivan. (Perhaps I already sent a copy? If so, please pass this along to someone who'll treasure it.) One need not read Sulivan straight through. I start and stop anywhere to meditate on his meditations.

It is lovely and cool here this summer. A heavenly fog hangs around until early afternoon, by which time nothing can heat up too greatly. My dear roses are happy, and the tree-frogs are whizzing about.

Peace to you —

H.

P.S. Have you heard anything along the following lines:

A while ago someone described Mary as our Perfect Mother — available to anyone who doesn't *have* a mother (i.e., loses one, has an abusive one, and so on). I forgot the story, but it struck me so sweetly. What a good idea — a generic Perfect Mother.

Mary as our Perfect Mother

If you have a line of text about that somewhere, it would be handy to include in my new book. All that's in my files is one clipping of a short prayer by Mother Teresa: *"Mary, Mother of Jesus, be a mother to each one of us."* Lovely, no?

(I thought recently, while writing that book on childhood, that *every* child's mother at her best actualizes some dimension of Mary which is another reason the Perfect Mother seems a universal archetype.)

A Spiritual Friendship

July 1996
(Letter Excerpt)

Dear MF:

I agree totally with you that Love in prayer (prayer of the heart? prayer without ceasing?) — whatever we call it — leads to completion, no matter what the outer husks of our creaturely appearance seem. Julian of Norwich is one saintly sort who acknowledges this:

On Julian and completion

> *I saw that in God our nature is complete and that He is never displeased with the life He has chosen.*

For several years now, especially before sleep, a prayerful meditation occurs now as *hesychia*,* the Prayer of the Heart. I'm drawn into a deep, acute tranquility. Something about sleep also brings on a profound peace (could that be a foretaste of what we call death?). I consider this peace a grace, the greatest blessing, but — and here is my point — *having absolutely nothing to do with personal virtue*. That is, I've done nothing to earn it, or "deserve" this. Again and again "person" fails, but God's Presence lifts one up, lets one keep going, bolstered in God ... so, once more paraphrasing Meister Eckhart, "Honor belongs to God" — who has honored God?

Those who have wholly gone out of themselves, [24] and who do not look above, beneath or beside themselves, and whose lives give joy to those who are in everlasting life (i.e., the angels and saints). As Jesus said, "The prince of this world comes but finds nothing in me." (Or words to that effect.)

Inward listening

Life in a hermitage: Don't ask what, exactly, this means. I hasten to discern by inward listening. After a certain point in this walk, if we're on the wrong track, we know it by virtue of the Holy Spirit alive, in us. As we read in Revelation, "And here is the Mind which hath Wisdom."

---

* Note to reader: hesychia, tranquility or stillness, is "linked through its Greek root with the idea of being seated, fixed and so concentrated." See The Philokalia, compiled by St. Nikodimas of the Holy Mountain and St. Makarios of Corinth, Vol. 1, London, The Eiling Trust, 1979, pp. 14-15.

July

Recalling one of your earlier remarks, I also get on others' nerves (and they get on mine, Big Time). Nevertheless, I don't worry much about this or huff and puff after worldly standards of perfection. After all, I can never fulfill these outer measures anyway as they're twisted inside-out.

Perhaps I should say in the scheme of eternity, whatever we mortals do without God doesn't matter much — like your priest friend told you at that wishing well in Rome: *"It doesn't matter, Sister, which way we throw the coin ..."*

I suspect our intense desire for completion in, or union with, God is rooted in God's Presence: We love, because, first, we are loved — because, first, God loves us: We are complete in One Who is All completeness, the head of all power and principality, "For in him dwells all the fullness of the Godhead bodily." [25] Not we "will be," "could be" or "ought to be." By faith and grace, we are. (Wasn't it Pascal who wrote that desire for oneness with God is evidence of a holy Reality?) *Col. 2: 10*

That same Reality disposes me to solitude and silence. I love Theresa of Lisieux's observation: That frequently it happens that a mother has one child who is weaker or more willful than her others, but the greater spendthrift she is in loving, the greater her love for the one in most need of her care and solicitude. (I *think* it was Theresa — I get her and Teresa of Avila mixed up sometimes.) Along these lines, St. Theresa of Lisieux's thought for the day buoys one up — although I can't recall where this comes from (probably Beevers' *Storm of Glory*), *St. Theresa of Lisieux*

> *I sought to find in Holy Scripture some suggestion [of how I might be uplifted] and came across these words ... "Whosoever is a little one, let him come to me" ... but wishing further to know what he would do to the "little one," I continued my search and this is what I found: "You shall be carried ... as one whom the mother caresseth, so will I comfort you" ... Our failings themselves ought not to lessen our trust.* [26]

"Of my own self I can do nothing:" You know, we sense that God bestows a great deal of love on us, and by virtue of that recognition, our own love increases along with trust in completion, in God. Our true nature is complete because God's infinite goodness is unbounded. I am His workmanship. I know that because God knows me. This is in my heart.

By the by, that *let it go* line you liked is from an e.e. cummings' poem of the same name. [27]

Do keep your letters and tapes coming. I suspect our dialogue on completion has just begun and welcome all your perceptions.

As you always say, Shalom,

H.

P.S. What did you think of that last radio interviewer? She was a crusty nut, no? You heard, at the start of that tape, my knee-jerk rudeness. Just the sound of her voice irritated me. Some voices are like that.

August
TOWARD A UNIVERSAL SANCTITY

*H*OT SUMMER MONTHS *prompt not lazier letters but more intense and lengthier communiqués. The August exchanges reflect the two friends' sustained interest in ideas profoundly religious. For example, they discuss ...*

- *Can one actually gain the Mind of Christ?*
- *How do we develop fidelity (i.e., consciously-made commitment) develop?*
- *What does it mean to be a "seeker" or a true contemplative?*

Gratefulness guides each friend to the region of her own, distinctive eloquence, and this cycle of letters gives us a look into the state of mind of those who live their faith, spontaneously and without legalism.

Whether one is becoming more assertive or learning what it means to "honor father and mother" or growing in an impersonal love that feels an illogical compassion in the face of seeming human weakness, a spiritual friendship encourages the conversion of daily experience into universal patterns of sanctity.

A Spiritual Friendship

As noted elsewhere, the friends frame their most mundane concerns in spiritual terms. For them, this is no intellectual exercise, no trendy technique by which to reach an idealized human perfection, not a response to authoritarian others or to some law — merely the delicate unfolding of transcendent Reality actualizing itself concretely.

August

August 15, 1996

Dear MF:

According to your recent tape (which I'm enjoying while driving around and for which I thank you), your quiet, encouraging voice tells me you're away this week. By the time you get this, you'll have visited with your brother. I trust your time away was fulfilling? You're probably happy to get home again, too. Your remarks about our distant friendship meant so much, and I thank you, feeling much the same — as if I have a sister in Christ. Your sharing the correspondence between St. Clare and Agnes was edifying. Yes, I, too, consider our exchanges — your tapes and my occasional written remarks — making for an interesting book. Once I nearly put something together to surprise you but got bogged down by other writing. Ah well. (A project for the 21st century.)

*Re*reading my memoir through your eyes, I see that it is primarily friends in spirit who encourage me. Not, I'm obliged to add, family. With the exception of my relationship with my grandmother, my happiest days came when I finally extricated myself from the family nest and the sway of its influence. That took some doing. And although I was as loving and kind as possible, what is loving and kind to me can seem unloving and unkind to others. Sulivan adds a word or two about that in his book — about keeping parenting short — and I love him for it.

Friends in Spirit

From *Love's* vantage point, reconciliation is ever-present — there is nothing but love. Your comments about Mary leading us to Jesus were wonderful and I shall replay that portion of tape again. In my case, a circuitous route led me to Mary: In childhood, I had the closest imaginable relationship with God (probably some mystical oneness) without support from my environment. I actually disobeyed my parents' wishes (two kindly, but sophisticated and anti-religious intellectuals) for any semblance of religious life. In adulthood after a long dry spell, those peak religious experiences returned. At about age 29 or 30, the Mind of Christ became real, experiential. Promptly thereafter, I became a Christian. Beholding all from the Mind of God, how could one not? Finally, after a

On the leadings of Mary

A Spiritual Friendship

year or two of studying Scripture, Mary's compassionate spirit became the archetypal and actual perfect Mother, as mentioned. One of Bernard of Clairvaux's biographers says, "The Son harkens to the Mother; the Father harkens to the Son." But that seems greatly intellectualized — a law too linear and far too divided for me to comprehend. God *is* simultaneously our Perfect Mother *and* Father, no? In God, who harkens or flies about here and there?

On keeping parenting short

Anyway, I resonate with Sulivan's urging that parenting is not a lifetime job. Your relationship with your mother, on the other hand, is truly enviable. You two must have ridden the same spiritual wavelength.

No divisive elements in Heaven

Both branches of my family were riddled with intermarrying couples, and my family represents the world, nearly all the major religions. By mutual accord they rejected religion. When I became a Christian, my mother said, "That's nice, dear, just be careful not to take it too seriously." Sigh. So I develop my faith and leave all other divisive elements of manmade creed to be settled in eternity. Paul taught we can receive the weak in faith without engaging in "*doubtful disputations*" (Rom. 14: 1), for the Kingdom is not meat, drink or debate but peace, righteousness and joy in the Holy Ghost (Rom. 14: 17). In Heaven, only the purest reconciliation exists. Right? Anyway, it's absolutely certain that in God there is no division. None.

The Bulletin of Monastic Interreligious Dialogue handles these interfaith issues so beautifully.[28] The books I am collecting these days for the hermitage strictly relate to the *Mind* of Christ (i.e., wherein "none are *Jews, Greeks or Romans,*" etc.). If you can come up with classic titles I should purchase, do let me know.

Mind of Christ

This Mind of Christ occupies all my waking thought. That radical, unitive consciousness is the *only* thing happening, the only Reality. Like completion: Only the saints understand because only they view everything from the standpoint of God; only they encourage us to believe completion exists for *us*. St. Teresa of Avila once wrote that it was a torture to have a spiritual director so inexperienced that he grew anxious the instant she introduced such topics. Any out of the ordinary

August

experience upset him. By contrast, Merton's *New Man* is so marvelously consoling about all this and reinforces completely Col. 3: 15, namely that we not only can, but must *"put off the old man and put on the new."* His sentiments reveal why, one day, he'll be recognized as a great modern Saint.

Christ's words, *"Whoso shall deny me before men, him will I also deny before my Father which is in Heaven,"* say to me that we must do more than simply give utterance to our faith. We must actually live it. This living is Abraham's *works*, no? — and the purest pleasure and the most exquisite challenge.

Without that foundational, intuitive knowing (born of the Mind of Christ), without chewing up Scripture and other encouragements for reinforcement on that single, elemental point, I don't see how anyone manages. I can hardly utter one word on the issue without expressing myself poorly. Ah but Oswald and Andrew — now there were two who knew.*

Sorry to ramble. Something you said on your tape drew this out.

Once more: Your kind remark about our distant friendship is reciprocated in feeling, with thanks for all your support,

Love in Christ,

H.

---

* Refers to authors Oswald Chambers and Andrew Murray, mentioned previously.

A Spiritual Friendship

August 1996
(Transcribed Tape)

Shalom, H,

I'm responding to two earlier letters, not really having had time to write until today.

Personal asides

I am pleased you like my voice on tape. Many people say when I proclaim the scriptures, the reading at Mass, that my speaking voice is soothing. You can tell I am not a professional speaker. I pause so frequently. What I like about your tapes is that, in interviews, you don't come across like a speaker who knows it all. Your voice is so pleasant, really easy on the ears. Sister M noticed the same thing, so we have a mutual admiration society going here.

Completion and commitment

As to your remark about convent life and completion: You are so right. Convent life, per se, doesn't bring one to completion. Obedience to our vocation (whatever it is — parenting or medicine or single life); faithfulness; the never-wavering commitment carries us to completion. I like that. Choosing toward God in utter faithfulness, we move toward completion.

Long ago, the words of Gabriel Marcel, the Christian existentialist, struck a similar chord with me. Marcel says that whether we commit ourselves to religious life or to a spouse in married life or to single life or anything else, we make those vows in the present — while thinking rationally. We know this choice is what we want. In the future, when our emotions tempt us to throw in the towel, we remember our promise, made when we were fully aware, recall it in the present and that memory carries us through distressful times into the future. Being faithful to the commitment means putting our hand to the plow. We do not turn back.

When a friend of mine was ordained, he wrote the following on his card:

> *God calls us to Himself, not to torture us but to fill us with good, so full of His goodness that we splash it out to others within splashing distance.*

On "never wavering"

That's not an accurate quote, but it's close and I like it:

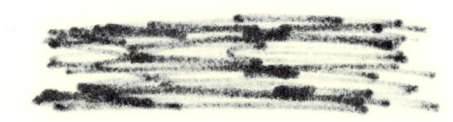

August

God summons us to infuse our life with Love. Being faithful to a vocation and "never wavering" means to fill up with the love and goodness of God and let that spread, first into every facet of our life, as it's said — you know, "do what you love." We build a life we value, and then — secondly, we spread our joy to others. When you build a life you want and love it, that's manifested commitment. And it's not always easy. Everything you desire doesn't automatically flow to you in a straight line. Yet, through the discipline of life — the school of life — we learn mysteriously that we have what we desire. We're both saying much the same thing.

I pick up through your writings, tapes and disclosures that you, too, have made that commitment to the Lord and that you have chosen Him as your portion and your cup. Though, as you say, you've placed one foot in the world and one in this Paradise of Heaven. That is the perfect life: To remain aware of the world, yet serve God. Even here in the convent we sustain that awareness. You must do so even more since you walk more freely than I do in my enclosed life. And I sense all that — that you have consciously chosen that.

No turning back

Is it your experience that, once you set sail on this obedient journey, there's no turning back? It's that going toward the Utter East that C. S. Lewis writes about. Always moving toward the Son. You don't *want* to go back because nothing desirable is back there anymore. Your work suggests you've experienced that. That's what I mean, too: That this vocational life, this religious journey, is my portion. I couldn't turn back — maybe for a while, but then everything would turn to straw.

When I experience others living through tragedy, illness or death and then turning to us for prayers, I realize all that matters in the end is the life we live in God and for others, but in God. For instance, I just received word that a school friend recently died of lung cancer. She was relatively young for this day and age, but smoked a lot. She left five children (most of them married now). Her husband called me knowing she and I were friends. Even though I had not heard from him before this, he begged for prayers for himself and for her.

Prayers during tragedy

When trouble comes right down to the wire, people turn to

53

God. This earthly life renders us more aware. Not only do we here pray for our own relatives, friends and people we know, but then each Sister here has her own circle that we hear about, and then people phone our Monastery to request our help. We are fully aware of the tragedies and sadness of life — frequently more than the joys — and realize how fragile life is. Even within all that, we sustain a joyful community.

Often people come here either seeking the cloistered life or, because they are in religious life and simply like to be with the community. We sit with them at tea and talk a little during meals (not at breakfast but at dinner and supper). (Only those in religious life may enter the cloister to share some time with us.)

On assertion

Quite right: We need to say something when others hurt us, in as kindly a way as possible. I told my spiritual director that, over the long haul, I've become more outspoken. I'm glad of that. There is a time to speak and a time to keep silent, and I weigh my words before I do speak, but yes — one needs to say something ...

I enjoyed your saying that your assertiveness seems to be more spontaneous, if also causing you to blunder your way into "little truths that need to be released." I loved your expression. That's exactly how I'd put it. Like blundering my way into little truths because, you know, the truths I'm speaking are no big, Save-Bosnia-deal — no vision of peace for the world. Just these little verities, right here, documenting my small corner of the cosmos. And I love that you say these *need* to be released.

On holding oneself in

Often, when I say my Psalms and morning prayers or read Scripture, I find one I particularly love. For example, recently from Isaiah:

> *I say nothing — holding myself in like a woman in labor, panting and gasping.*

Isaiah told us exactly what he felt. Sometimes that's how I feel. I say nothing. I hold myself in, but then if the truth comes out, it's released. I love your line. That's precisely how I feel.

Encouragement along the religious way

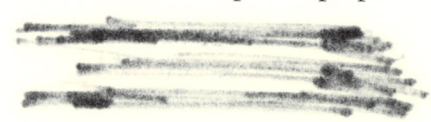

You asked about examples of people who have encouraged

August

me along. One incident (which didn't happen to me directly) involved, and was typical of, Sister MT who just died in May. The Sisters tell this story: Some friars, a group of novices, visited her while she was sick. Sister MT was very tiny, and when seated, positioned low to the ground. She had spinal problems and her back was bent. So she really sat very low. I guess these novice-friars were standing up tall, looking down at her. One young friar, sort of on the pious side, folded his hands and inquired, "Now, Sister, having lived this life a long, long time, could you give us some words of wisdom?" Sister MT looked up at him with her big brown eyes, pondering his question for a while, then replied, "Lighten up."

On lightening up

I just love that story. Sister MT would tell you something hilarious when you were serious or sad and least expecting it, just to make you laugh. I discovered her great sense of irony, and that incident made me laugh. She's right: We get too serious. We've got to lighten up. Especially those of us who seek the religious way.

Formal vs. informal spirituality

Yesterday we were sitting at the table with a couple of young guests who are interested in the religious life. They're exceedingly pious. Sometimes some visitors sew pictures of religious figures on their clothes and present themselves in an extremely devout fashion. They may exemplify a return to a pious, more devotional spirituality.

Our Abbess tells us that earlier in the decade many Sisters entered the cloistered life believing in religious visions of Mary, the Blessed Mother. Those Sisters had an intense, traditional spirituality — a devotional pattern that occurred in different locations, all over the United States. Then our generation came along, what with our Vatican II spirituality, and we evolved a religious life with less emphasis on externals. We read Calvin and Hobbs cartoons (wherever God is present), and things became much freer. Our Abbess says that now a new generation is entering religious life with a return to that more devotional spirituality. Younger people visit, find us reading a joke book for leisure, and wonder, "Where did they learn their spirituality?" The pendulum has swung back. What goes around comes around, full circle.

Dialogue on completion

You say that to you "completion" means that stirring of

life, light and love of God — living waters in us through Christ. And you write *"in us."* What I've learned from you is that there is a living supranatural source within us. It's *in* there, and we must bring it forth. Because of that, now, frequently I speak out, think my own thoughts and bring them out. I learned that from you, which was a grace in my life. It involves self-forgetting. Isn't that true? Self-forgetting I learned about from Father H, in Denver.

"Get ahead of the selfish ones"

Once I told Father H the following story: When I was a Sister of Charity, two of us, another Sister and I, went up to a Jesuit-owned mountain cabin and really scrubbed it clean. The Jesuits let us visit and use it (I think with the unstated aim of having us clean it). No one would have wanted to sleep there, it was so disheveled. Sister B and I scoured everything until it sparkled. We used so much water that when Sister B took her shower at night, she used up the last bit of water. There was no water left in the well for me, not even cold water, not even a few drops to brush my teeth. I was filthy. When I told Father H that I almost got mad at her because of this, he replied, "That's what we must do: Get ahead of those selfish ones." That was a learning experience for me.

I often repeat that same line here: "Let's do something quickly — to get ahead of those selfish ones!" Of course, what's actually occurring is that *I'm* the selfish one scurrying to get ahead. Father H's casual joke has stayed with me all these years. Real love is self-forgetful. We forget ourselves completely, in God, on behalf of others — and we do not strain to measure how much we have or where we are with God. In your letter, you write that love is God's activity *in* us and that that's the point of human completion — to disappear in God's love.

On seekers drawn by Love

You also say you don't consider the word "seeker" to be accurate for those who are disappearing like that. Correct. That's not "seeking." We live in God and He in us. No separation whatsoever. Constant presence. Quite right. I know what you mean, the word "seeker" seems to imply one who runs after gurus, fad meditations or trendy workshops.

You are looking in *fruit*ful gaze. I relate to that expression, too. It's as expressed in the Cloud of Unknowing, which I

August

never really could read; yet one line from the Cloud has stayed with me: the cloud of unknowing is pierced with a dart of Love. That seems to be as you've said: fruitful gaze. Eye and ear only to God. That's exactly what I mean when using the word seeking. We're always throwing out this dart of loving attention to this cloud of unknowing. Always gazing, ear and eye only to God — as you say, foregoing all others for Christ's spirit alive in us. Whenever I use the word seekers, it's not meant to imply those who run from workshop to workshop or to guru after guru, but who turn eye and ear toward God and who actually find him. Sinetar's book on film and spirituality proposes that even movies reflect God and therefore teach us about love. So actually, when we are seeking God, everything in us speaks to him and speaks to us of God.

I loved your quotation from Julian of Norwich:

> *I saw that in God our nature is complete, that he is never displeased with the life he has chosen.*

On Julian's idea of completion

That is really beautiful. Love is what draws us, and all things work together for those who love God. Even our faults, our lapses, whatever. He's not displeased, I'm sure of that, if we are tending to be open and sincere with him. I've seen that in my own life, right here.

I see that you rest in Him and have that deep tranquility about which Julian speaks, yet you say this has nothing to do with your own virtue — that you've done nothing to "earn" or deserve that rest. You say it's a grace, an undeserved kindness or a blessing, and that you experience that profoundly, especially at night — before sleep. I feel the same way — so blessed and frequently at night.

On grace and blessings

When I put my head down on the pillow at night, I sleep soundly knowing I am blessed in so many ways. In some respects, life hasn't been easy, but God has certainly blessed me richly. That's what you're saying, too: That you experience being loved and blessed. What else could we ask for?

On one of Thomas Merton's tapes for novices he says, "Today's my 20th anniversary, and let me tell you, it takes 20 years just to get used to the monastic life." That is so true. I've been here 21 years and experience the truth of his remark.

Time in the religious life

A Spiritual Friendship

I'm only beginning to know what I can say, what not to say, what to do, and not do and coming to terms with this life. This knowledge has brought me peace. And it does bring peace to those around me.

On life in a hermitage

I love what your Japanese friend told you: That within us exist three, interconnected spaces: Personal, social and holy space, and that maybe one way to God is simply to enlarge our "holy space," the open, inner field. As for you moving toward life in hermitage, yes, that sounds appealing. Even to me. I do have certain conditions for that here. Sometimes, just as Merton yearned to live in a hermitage, so do I. Our call here is not to a life of a hermit. We are called to fraternity and life in community. We do have spaces to go for retreat, to live by ourselves, and I see where that hermitage life is very appealing. One motive for my coming here was to simplify life, as Henry David Thoreau wrote about in *Walden*. Reading *Walden* I thought, "I'd like to live a simpler life," and that impulse carried me here.

On holy beer

One thing I've found — I don't know if I'll express this accurately, but I'll say it: One goes through a period of seeking God through prayer or mystic writers (not, as discussed, in the sense of chasing gurus or anything). It's intense. Then one returns again to a very natural process and generates new growth from that. I've discovered that the mystics are very down-to-earth about all this. Merton underscores this point as he tells of a college student who wanted to meet him and traveled to Merton's hermitage. He found Merton down by a creek, sitting alone, drinking a bottle of beer. And the student grew disillusioned. Merton did not fit his idea of a holy person. But, to me, even with his bottle of beer, Merton was holy.

A true contemplative

Elsewhere Merton wrote that a true contemplative is not someone who looks down at the person in the gutter and says, "I'll help you up out of that gutter." The contemplative is the one who is *in* the gutter, with the other guy. That's compassion. I like that. I know there is no crime that I am incapable of committing. I once remarked to my spiritual director that I understood why people kill others. He laughed. But at times, I also experience rage and that makes me realize that we all have basic instincts and basic desires. We all are alike

August

in some fashion, all flawed. Even in that we find our redemption: That a weak, imperfect human being could be loved by God, could be good for others, and be a grace for them is the work of God — God working through us.

It was heartening to hear that you, too, get on other people's nerves and that you feel selfish and imperfect. You don't come across like that. In your talks I hear you bending to others. Like with that one interviewer from Rhode Island or someplace, who was edgy and cross — even though you *felt* ill-tempered, I didn't sense that. Your saving grace is that you don't worry too much about yourself. Like my priest friend said when he saw me hesitate before tossing a coin into the Trevi Fountain in Rome, "It doesn't matter, Sister, which way you throw the coin." That's so true. I really do try to remember that. That's such a beautiful thought. That's why I wrote the *Victor of Life*: *

Self-forgetting and holiness

> It doesn't matter, Sister,
> Which way you throw the coin,
> Life happens just the same.
>
> Fountains of life, rivers of joy,
> Streams of sorrows,
> Flow through time counted out,
> Leading us on the path to the other shore.
> The Upward journey, the passing spiral of life,
> Slips into death.
> It doesn't matter, Sister, (or Brother)
> Which way you throw the coin,
> Death happens just the same.
> But Christ, our Life, has conquered.
> We, the stars and everything else in between,
> Become a New Creation.
> The Risen, Cosmic Christ,
> The Alpha and the Omega, is Victor
> Of our Life.

---

* Dedicated to Bishop Daniel Walsh and Bishop Joseph Charron, September 1994. (Copyright to the poem held by the poet.)

A Spiritual Friendship

There is a wonderful spiritual direction that teaches us not to worry so much about worldly images — for example, how we come across to others. Being inclined to get wrapped up in what others say — part of the occupational hazard here — I continually work on that.

Loving the weak ones

You wrote the mother who looks after her weaker child spends more love on that child. As a teacher, you probably experienced the same thing: The students who gave you the most trouble are those you remember. In the long run, we teachers come to love them more. I never thought of that before, but since you brought it up, the ones who were troublesome, naughty or demanding I remember to this day — even their names, and their turn-about, too; how they came through with the lessons, their learning, their improved conduct. It was wonderful to watch them grow and improve.

Personal asides

I took a trip home to Ohio where my brother and his wife live. The Abbess lets me go home; it's a wonderful opportunity. Most of the Sisters don't get to do this because they're from around here, so their families come here. My brother is a dairy farmer and neither he nor his wife can get away.

Your P.S. made me laugh: Very funny that you called the interviewer "a crusty nut." I love that phrase and your self-description of "knee-jerk rudeness." I have that knee-jerk rudeness, too.

Your St. Theresa thought for the day is helpful. Somewhere in scripture, maybe it was in James, we read, "Cast your care upon the Lord because he cares for you." I love that line, don't you? It's the same thing: He'll carry us because he cares for us.

So, lots of shalom and thank you for your long letter and for your e.e. cummings poems. That let-it-all-go poem is just beautiful, especially the line, *"the smashed word broken."* Thank you so much. You inspire me to persist in piercing the cloud of unknowing. Or, what was that other thing you said? Same thing: To gaze heavenward with *"fruitful gaze."*

Peace,

M.F.

WomanWell
1784 La Crosse Avenue
St. Paul, Minnesota 55119-4808

September
IMPROVED EFFECTIVENESS

*C*HRISTIAN MYSTICS *move actively in consciousness from the Infinite to the definite. Not passive types, they aspire to infinitize life and to define Infinity and actualize the Transcendent in their waking consciousness.*[29]

Mystics tend to reject the fictive boundaries of egoisms and the small self. To them, the strong faith referred to in scripture is no theory but ever-present substance. Thus someone like Abhishiktananda, the Western contemplative mentioned earlier, could testify to the way faith supports activity:

> The life of every individual and especially of the Christian, is one of prayer and contemplation springing from faith in the holy Presence. This faith is the very life-breath of spiritual people. In the Spirit their spirits live and breathe, as their bodies live and breathe in the air that surrounds them. In each of their acts, whether physical or mental, they as it were breathe in and breathe out the Spirit who fills all things within and without; they continually draw him in, and continually give him out, for human life means the constant acceptance of the gift of God. [30]

A Spiritual Friendship

Sister MF's September note illustrates how her contemplative Order breathes life into their religious vows: They cultivate a wholesome relationship with one another. They set aside time to assess their individual contribution to the collective good. Each examines her own heart – motives, attitudes, deeds – as it affects the context of community life.

H's interpretation of such topics as forgiveness and the Parable of the Wheat and Tares or her sense of God as intensely present just prior to the night's sleep underscores the way the Transcendent dominates the mystic's normal awareness: Love alone infuses thought and undergirds action with divine energy.

We note repeatedly that spiritual ardor improves – rather than lessens – effectiveness, since God is the driving consideration behind routine activity. John Chrysostom, a patriarch of Constantinople and "patron of preachers" (c. 347-407) once noted the inherent Divinity in the disciples' preaching,

> *... how else could twelve uneducated men, who lived on lakes and rivers and wastelands, get the idea for such an immense enterprise? How could men who perhaps had never been in a city or a public forum think of setting out to do battle with the whole world?* [31]

September

September 20, 1996

Dear H,

Peace and every blessing.
A quick note:

We read your article in that national magazine. Sister M gave it to me after reading it. It is good and it challenges. But then your writing does that for me. — *On books and articles*

The other book you sent, *Morning Light* by Jean Sulivan is also good, but not quick going. However, as it is profound, I am reading it slowly.

Another book I picked up in Boston is *Aging as a Spiritual Journey*. It is insightful and emphasizes issues that you have already dealt with: Changing careers and adopting a more contemplative dimension in life. The author, Eugene Bianchi, explores both psychology and religion. Again, slow reading.

I'm listing a few questions we've been asked to ponder during an upcoming retreat — our own reflections on community: — *On community*

- What is Community for you?
- What kind of Community person are you?
- How do you contribute to build community?
- How can we, as individuals, improve community life?

As you see, I am learning the computer. The enclosed card was designed on it.

Much love and shalom, shalom,

MF.

A Spiritual Friendship

September 17, 1996

Dear MF:

Thanks for your most recent missives. I particularly enjoyed your stories about your family — and your mother* — and would like to quote or paraphrase you in one of the last chapters of my book on childhood. I'll send you my edits for your approval as I'd love your feedback anyway.

On a pre-existing forgiveness

The thing is, the person I was no longer exists, so it's particularly tricky to reconstruct the emotions of childhood. Everything has been reconciled. In a sense, all forgiveness *is* — has *always* existed. This is *impersonal*, not at all respective of persons or specific situations. One need only be infused with the Holy Spirit to realize that *Love cannot but forgive*. Forgiveness is not really an issue *in* the God kind-of-love, since in God, in a Christly love, there is no memory of hurt or slight. Just love-consciousness: Love knows only Love. In my experience it's a certainty that eventually forgetting also comes. If Love has always been, is not reconciliation pre-existing, too?

On sleep and spirituality

Returning to our previous discussion about a heightened awareness of God before sleep, I read that St. Bernard believed a chaste soul loves solitude and night and bed. Often, when Bernard was completely exhausted, he continued to work with intense fervor and then, before sleep, experienced the Presence of God and the beneficence of prayer:

> *[The one] who wishes to pray in peace will take into account not only the place, but the time. The moment of rest is the most favorable and when nocturnal sleep establishes a profound silence everywhere, prayer becomes more free and more pure. Arise during the night and pour out your heart like water before the Lord ...* [32]

Doesn't this explain so much? The "human" sense lessens prior to sleep. I'm thankful for these lines.

I experienced a marvelous healing this weekend while

---

* Note to reader: Lost letters (or out of sequence). The topic of Sister MF's family returns in the last October letter.

September

rereading the Parable of the Tares and Wheat, a teaching about managing our attention. Rather than scrutinizing our circumstances for improvements, the parable instructs us to get our attention *off* "the tares." We are told not to *try* to rid ourselves of tares, lest we root up the good seed along with the tares. Only at harvest-time should we bundle up the tares, burn them once and for all and bring the wheat into our Father's barn.

Parable of wheat and tares

One simply sustains the knowledge that the good seed *has been sown, is growing, is bearing* fruit without thought about a problem still existing. With strong faith in the harvest, anything else becomes irrelevant. What's important is *trust*, like that grand encourager Paul deJaegher wrote. Even while reading, faith in the "good seed" is heightened. Within a couple of days, my harvest was tangibly at hand. Neat, no?

Does this make sense? Usually these deep wisdoms wash over me as a wordless knowing that purifies everything: Either we change or the situation does.

Your lesson plan came. I so admire the title, *Build with Living Stones*. The art is beautiful, too, as are the short stories of St. Francis and St. Clare. And I love the concept of "the world as monastery." Of course, that's really *it*, no?

Personal asides

I'm searching for words to describe the focus of my little collection of hermitage books, should you have ideas. Father M (a Basilian) in Canada is a great ongoing support. He has sent me wonderful books — one classic on St. Basil; two Merton first editions and fine editing ideas. The books and research emphasize the Mind of Christ, but my current Board of Directors (particularly a couple) suggests secular terms to describe this for broader — corporate — appeal. I sense it's time for me to plod on alone, without committees and such. I mean, really ...

Your first unit's lesson of *Build with Living Stones* shows that it's inspiring enough to tell one's truth simply, in gentle, nonjudging terms. Then let the chips fall where they may. Anyway, I welcome your thoughts on the hermitage's focus.

Peace and all blessings,

H.

A Spiritual Friendship

September 25, 1996

Dear H,

Peace and blessings.

Thank you for your recent letter and, yes, you can use anything about my mom that I taped for you. I am always flattered that you are touched by my ramblings.

Julian of Norwich on forgiveness

About forgiveness: You are right on target in saying, "Love cannot *but* forgive." In line with this, today we had a workshop on Julian of Norwich and her book *Showings*. I could not get into this book, until Father V opened it up for us. He provided wonderful insights about this anchorite (1342-1426) whose theology Merton loved. Related to your thought about love: Julian said we cannot anger God by sin because God has no wrath. He is always Love.

Parable of wheat and tares

Julian of Norwich presents the same idea (but slightly differently) as you did with your insight on the parable of the wheat and the tares. She says this matter of faith is like baking a cake: Your intention is to bake the cake and maybe you make a mess of the kitchen (drop things and so on), but since your purpose is to bake a cake, somehow it turns out. All the distractions and hindrances work themselves out in the end, the harvest of the wheat. Yes, the good seed wins the day and all for good.

Take encouragement from Julian. Her book was lost for years and only recently found to be of any note.

It is hard to articulate those spiritual moments, but I know what you're saying. I have been there and it is flat in the telling because no one can capture the living beauty of it all. Right?

Here's one idea for the name of your hermitage collection: All spiritual traditions have mountain experiences, so something like Mount Hope, Mount Faith, and so on might work. My favorite is Mount Hope.

Shalom,

MF.

October
A SPIRIT OF ONENESS

*T*HE DEMOCRATIC *character structure of a spiritual friendship must account for some of the optimism and subjective fulfillment of these conversations. Trust and a true meeting of minds blesses the friends, or as one of them told us, "We began to feel everyone deserves a spiritual friendship — probably longs for one — you know, a nonintrusive link to, or oneness with, someone kind and constant and nonjudgmental who's in your corner."*

The term empty relationship refers to connections that lack intimacy and meaning. A spiritual friendship — however infrequently the companions may see one another face-to-face — is, by contrast, made richer because of intimacy, truth telling and shared, compelling purposes. As we see, there is nothing complicated about such sharing. Everything — little garden life and the simplest tasks — gives spiritual friends a reason to rejoice because, in them, everything works harmoniously to reveal God.

For example, as each friend faces some trial, she discusses it openly with the other, yet in a manner that lessens self-pity and somehow generates inexpressible joy. On the face of it, this makes no logical sense until we recall St. Therese de Lisieux's lighthearted words, "We are too little to be able always to rise above difficulties. Well, then, let us pass beneath them quite simply." [33]

Her remark underscores the inherent good humor in every vividly spiritual life.

The supposed hardship also offers spiritual friends an opportunity to pray for one another. In stillness and the poise of love, they strengthen their own faith. Seeming obstructions tend to bring believers closer together in a spirit of oneness (as with these two) rather than driving a wedge of isolation between them.

It is not the physical distance between us and our friends that makes us lonely but emotional distance: Our feeling that we are alone or misunderstood. Separation is impossible when one lives in Love.

Oswald Chambers elaborates on the idea of transcending trials when he writes, *"The surf that distresses the ordinary swimmer produces in the surf-rider the super-joy of going clean through it."* [34]

October

October 2, 1996

Dear MF:

Peace to you with thanks for your tape of last month. (I'm leaving on a land scouting trip, so both this and my next letter may be tardy.) Your boat photo is lovely. Haunting. Here, in turn, a more "grounded" picture (excuse the pun) of my local General Store, open for business since the late 1800s. The owners are old timers, real pioneers. Rural country folk who own huge plots of rolling coastal acreages nearby, as well as the white washed Post Office building (and the land it sits on) across the street. (See the flag and flag post by the driveway?) Now you get a better idea of how remote it is here. I love it: The fog, the sea, the forests, the works.

Back to Julian: As a mystic she seems typically oceanic, typically unpretentious. Julian expresses herself so simply. She helps me clarify a certain supernatural and inexpressible communion. The characteristic of all Saints: Whatever their doctrinal heritage, they reflect God, draw us to God — not to themselves. They unify with their words, and "while they are yet speaking," God hears. Sometime ago (when we exchanged ideas on the matter of trust) I sent you one of Julian's quotes to advance my notion of completeness. Like you, I love Julian's acceptance of our completion in God. Few theologians have the clarity to expand on that issue and seem too worldly-wise to think God's thoughts about us.

Characteristics of Saints

Tauler — a spiritual advisor I love in small doses — is practically a bookkeeper as he catalogues our flaws. I repeatedly turn to Tauler for spiritual direction, then shut the book feeling more convicted of sin than led to God. (In his eyes, one is tainted; in Julian's eyes, one is a potential saint.) By contrast, St. Paul (no slouch on the topic of sin) leads one straight to Christ; as he insists wherever the Spirit of the Lord is there is liberty — the veil completely dissolves in the light of Christ (II Cor. 3: 14+).

Saints See Potential

Julian knows our spiritual liberty is assured, is *never* opposed and that any seeming opposition, or fleshly resistance to completion is taken up by Christ, and all of it — every microscopic bit — turned to Love's profit. Julian's experience of God as Love seems an absolute given.

Only the greatest mystics and saints encourage in this way, like Jacob Boehme who wrote that to see God's Light in our soul, we must keep our eye on the spirit, our attention out of *things* (i.e., the world) and simply be with God. Neat, yes?

Thanks for your recommendation of *Showings* which I ordered from Paulist today. I'm grateful you brought that volume to my attention. I wonder if it is any different than her *Revelations*.

What else can you recommend on anchorites?

Have you read *Dwelling Place for God* (Panikkar)? One of my dearest books. Bro. H, a Cistercian, recommended it, and I'm so appreciative that he did. Please consider browsing through it. It's a harder read than *Morning Light*, but so profoundly lavish, so universal. Extremely powerful. Talk about books that lift one up to the Mount of Hope ...

All peace,

H.

October

October 11, 1996
(Letter Excerpt)

Dear H,
Thanks for your last two letters.

I intended to write yesterday when I had a hunk of time but someone wanted to talk and we spent three hours on "stuff." All I did was basically stress that everyone here is striving. We're still human and our humanness shows. Anyway this letter is going to be rushed. *(Personal asides)*

Enclosed is a good article about the Anchorites' rule compared to Saint Clare and a bibliography that may help your research.

I love your picture of the General Store, and I've pictured your surroundings as such.

Stone by stone, step by step. Your second letter is heartening. It looks like you are moving forward on your hermitage dream.

There is a song from the film "Brother Sun and Sister Moon," something about doing things slowly, simply — step by step, stone by stone. That song speaks to me of our lives. We, too, are moving on our hope that we can build our monastery, stone by stone. *(Stone by stone)*

St. Clare added this word on being faithful:

> *The soul of a faithful man, who is the most worthy of all creatures, is through the grace of God surely made greater than the heavens.*

Another encouraging image I have is of St. Francis, praying before the Crucifix in San Damiano's Church in Assisi. That was when he heard God tell him, *"Rebuild my Church."* Francis took that direction literally and repaired that very church, asking stones from the townspeople. While he was redoing it, Francis yelled out to the people bringing stones: *"This church will house Poor Ladies who will be known for their holiness"* and today they are called Poor Clares. So that's my own lineage. Neat, no? *(A direction for St. Francis)*

Peace,

MF.

A Spiritual Friendship

October 17, 1996

Dear MF:

Please accept this modest gift for your Monastery's work, long overdue. Your card touched me. There are other reasons I was reminded to send along something in this mailing.

First, your letters have steadily encouraged me and have been mysteriously synchronous as well. Last month, when you wrote of Julian of Norwich, I had just completed a solitary reflective weekend wondering how I might mentor or be a sort of spiritual encourager to others while simultaneously scaling back my business, living as a "Desert Father." (Desert Mother? Was there such a thing?) Then came your reminder about Julian.

On spiritual friendship

And all along I feel your distant friendship is more perfect than many in the sense that it is a spiritual friendship — impersonal at its root and so grounded in our mutual living of a spiritual love in daily life, in concrete illustration of Christ.

I loved what Chambers says, that over and over God removes our friends in order to put Himself in their place "and that is where we faint and fail and get discouraged." [35] My first and favorite editor used to say that as we grow more Christly, God takes our toys away. She meant that in the light of Love, distractions dissolve and "this corruptible puts on incorruptible ... and death is swallowed up in victory." [36]

This is one important outgrowth of a dialogue like ours: Each uplifts the other while turning one's own mind progressively to that incorruptible "more perfect and greater" life. A spiritual friend speaks so as to advance the other's true life in Christ. So thank you.

Personal asides

The news of my newest manuscript is a mixed bag: The publishers love it, say it's the best thing I've written — "warm and loving" — *but* it lacks commercial draw. If I make it self-help, they'll gobble it up. God bless my agent for saying I'm becoming a decent writer and that this is decidedly not a self-help book, that I should be patient and that she'll find a home for it.

The paradox of obedience

Along with the turn toward a more contemplative life comes this turn in writing. I now simply trust that readers will

October

find their way to my books. I feel I've come to the end of my "commercial" life. My new life is hid with Christ in God (is that the scripture?), so I wait. Obscure as God's will often seems, doesn't it become evident through our knowing our deepest purposes? Stone by stone, right? God's compelling unfolds us in purposes that may seem cloudy even as we move toward them. We meet the paradox of that by faith, right? Georgia O'Keefe, the great painter, said she knew what to paint before she started. Otherwise, she just waited: "If there's nothing in my head, I do nothing." [37] Quite so.

You sound busy. I am as well but took a few days off as an early Fall retreat. Several times each year I structure an at-home, spiritual retreat for myself. This year, I cancelled my business trip back East and spent a glorious few days in stillness — and in my garden.

Say, if you can mail me a copy of *Spiritual Mothering* from Vol. 36, No. 7 of the *Cord* (or the journal itself), I'll be thankful.

Also, what's this about a duplicate book center? Do you want books for it?

Showings just arrived. I may review it. Its old publishing date (1971) will turn off most magazines. I received *Clare and the Ancren Riwle*, along with a book from a pal at Paulist on *Anchoress Spirituality*. So I have plenty to read.

All love in Christ,

H.

A Spiritual Friendship

October 1996
(Transcribed Tape)

Greetings, H,

Personal asides

I'm outside walking around the monastery wall, taping this letter to you. It's cool but sunny after the northeastern hit some areas around here. This time it didn't hit us. One struck before, a while back. Uprooted three big trees in the front, five in the back and cost us a pretty penny.

Well, Sister M got your message on the answering machine, and I'm sorry that I wasn't available. We were meeting with our lawyer about selling the building and the real estate. Whenever we have a meeting, we turn on the answering machine. Plus, the Franciscan Friars from nearby offered their cottage near the ocean to us, so we took our turns. It's really wonderful to go. I love the ocean, as you know.

On the Eucharist

Anyway, I'll explain what the card I sent meant: It is used during Mass. We believe that we can offer our prayers along with the Eucharist celebration — the infinite sacrifice of Jesus. We can pray for anybody or anything at that time, and especially at that time. That's the greatest of all prayers. Each day at Mass we have what we call petitions (after the gospel and before the offertory). It's really the liturgy of the Eucharist, and we offer petitions for anybody we want and always pray for all those who are good to us and all our friends and relatives. That's one of the petitions we say out loud. So our little card says that you will be included in all our masses.

Intercession and good works

Then there are good works: We believe that being kind to others or the daily work we do — like sweeping the floor — is a gift. These small acts can help save the world. I don't know if you go along with that, but what we do (and do well) in atonement for our own short-comings and for the world, God sees and is pleased as we unite our work with His beloved son. Then our daily office (which we say seven times a day) includes three Psalms and a prayer and a reading from the Bible. We also believe that as Moses stood up while the battle was going on and held his arms aloft to God for intercession: "Moses' hands were heavy, but others supported and steadied him." (Ex. 17:12) When we go to the office — the divine office, or

October

as it's called "the liturgy of the hours" — and hold up our breviary, we are interceding for the whole world. Sometimes I forget that. It's what we're really here for — to intercede for the whole world with our prayers.

I want to add that I feel that you are moving in such a beautiful direction. The Lord is really holding you in his hands and has a special care of you. Perhaps you feel that, too. I certainly sense it from what you say. Of course all that is between you and God. When I was in my first novitiate — this was the Sisters of Charity — we encountered this wonderful woman, Sister C, God rest her soul, who used to say, "Do not talk about anybody else's spiritual life because you may interfere with God." She also said, "Never discuss their prayer life because that's between them and God. And, don't give any advice." I've always remembered that. Yet I do feel that the Lord is working strongly in your life. I'm sure you sense that more than I do. I just wanted to say that, for what it's worth, and don't know how to express that on paper. So, I say it sort of face-to-face. Or ear-to-ear.

On the Lord's care

I'm sending along the book written by that interviewer who visited. Nobody here wanted to be interviewed, but finally a couple of us agreed. Later, she sent back the transcript-draft of the tape she made of our discussion. Sisters C and R didn't like what they said. Or they didn't like how they were edited and eventually declined the opportunity to be included in her book, saying "No" — they wanted nothing to do with it. I stuck with what I said, even knowing that I had started sentences and didn't finish them. I'm traveling all over the place when I talk. That's my intuitive nature.

Personal asides

I'm an INFP on the Meyers-Brigg inventory. That means "introvert," but in the M-B lexicon that's not one who withdraws from others but refers to a manner of making decisions. For instance, an extrovert on the M-B scale tends to jump into the deep water and *then* think about it, while an introvert sits on the bank by the water for a long while and thinks about it. And then jumps in. That's true for me. I'll sit on the bank 32 days (and that's a pretty high introvert) before jumping. Once I jump in, as you know, I stick to my decision. Like going to Poland — once I decided to go, I did it. I'm

Introverts, extroverts & communication

75

very high on the Intuitive scale. Intuitives see the wholeness of things: The beginning and the end. They frequently neglect to acknowledge the details in the middle. I do that when talking. The beginning is obvious, and I think everybody understands the middle, so I skip right on over to the conclusion.

To return to that interview: I seem scattered in my comments. When it was finally published, was I surprised. Many well-known people are included in it, like that Sister L who went to the Council, and Sister JC, who is a noted author and numerous others — all authorities of some sort. Then there's me — primarily because nobody else here wanted to be involved with the project (or those that tried dropped out).

I find by the time something of mine is published, I've already moved from my old position, and some of it I no longer feel. Basically it's me. I own it, but I might not express myself that same way if asked the same question today, at this point and time. I have to say I feel more at home with what I said in your memoir.

Personal asides

Forty-five minutes before the next bell rings, and I've got some work to do on the computer. While taping I'm walking around the yard. Maybe I sound a little winded? I've been walking around and taping this the whole time — correspondence and a little exercise at the same time. How efficient.

A young woman who plans to enter the monastery joined us while we were at the shore. She had breakfast with us one morning. (We ate huge breakfasts while we were there, bacon and eggs, which is a real treat. We usually just have bread or cereal here.) She came over after Mass. Since she works at a restaurant, at night time, she was able to join us for Mass at 8:00 a.m.

A friend of hers invited us out on their sailboat. Well, I must say I'm not fond of sailboats. However, this time we all went out on the sailboat in the late afternoon on a part of the bay that was very calm. Not even a ripple. I must admit, I enjoyed it. Her friend, knowing I feared the rocking of the boat, said, "I'm impressed. You must have prayed for this." It was a beautiful time. I had time to read and to reflect on the ocean, the fishermen out there and the sunrise. When I pick up my pictures, I'll send some of the sunrise which was gor-

October

geous. We watched Bill Moyers' first show on the Book of Genesis. It was terrific. I just loved it. Two Catholics, two Jewish people — one a rabbi — and others of other faiths shared their interpretations of Scripture and their beliefs, and I loved it — absolutely loved it. Generally, I don't have this time to talk to the Sisters, so when I share with you, it's wonderful to discuss what I'm most interested in: God.

Speaking of which, in *America* magazine I read about a man who did little else in life except read books and pray. He's 90 years old now. He spent all of his time just talking with people about God. When he rode in his car with others, he'd say, "We only talk about God in this car." Well, I, too, think everything leads to God. Boats and sea and ocean and trees and all of Nature speak of God. *Everything leads to God*

Hey, I better get going. I smile when I say, "Hey." It reminds me of a man (B) who worked here. B had three sisters who were nuns: one here, one in Memphis, one in Pennsylvania, and one in Evansville, Illinois. (That's four, isn't it? Yes: He had four sisters.) They were all Poor Clares. One, Sister MT — my friend — died a year ago May. Anyway, B was wonderful. He worked here for 65 years. Never married. But nice looking. I think he would have made a terrific husband for someone. Anyway, B used to talk to me, and once he started talking, you know, he kept on for quite a while. I'd listen and listen, and all of a sudden, he'd say: "Hey! Don't hold me up. Gotta go." *"Hey, gotta go," origins of*

So, I was going to say, "Hey! Don't hold me up! Gotta go." And *I'm* doing all the talking. This is a monologue.

Thank you for your call. I feel privileged that we have this relationship and honored that you care enough to share your thoughts with me. So lots of shalom and peace to you. Well, "shalom" and "peace" are the same thing — but "shalom" is more than peace, isn't it? It's the completeness of things — oh, the leaves are starting to fall. See what I mean? A real intuitive: Talking about peace, then I see some leaves and skip over to that topic! *On "shalom"*

Now, I do have to go in. I'm going toward the door and leaving the monastery garden. It's beautiful. I must send some pictures of the garden to you. It's more yard than gar-

A Spiritual Friendship

den, with lots of trees and not too many flowers. But a beautiful lawn.

So lots of shalom again, lots of shalom, H. And thanks again for your friendship.

MF.

October

October 25, 1996

Dear H,
Peace and every blessing.
Enclosed is a flyer for the book about women religious which I wrote about and also my interview.

On courage

When God leads us to Himself, all our insides are turned inside-out. That is the norm, so prepare yourself for battle. When I first came here and plunged deeper into the spiritual life, I thought I was losing my mind, but hang on; He will pull you through. Have courage, many have gone before you on this way. They will intercede for you.

What monks do

To your earlier remark about self-efforts and perfectionism, I came across an old story of a desert monk who was asked what the monks do all day in the monastery. He says, "Well, we get up and fall down. We get up and fall down." I love that line. So true.

Some say my interview remarks made it sound like the other Order did not pray. Oh, well. I am glad I am not in any public forum because I could not stand all this bickering about words and opinions. How do you survive?

You and your intentions are held in prayer.

Shalom,

MF.

A Spiritual Friendship

October 26, 1996

Dear MF:

Thanks for *The Cord*. The *Spiritual Mothering* article looks good, and I'll add a word about it at the end of this letter if there's time to scan it before mailing this. Do you want the magazine back? I read your interview. Most interesting and congratulations for your spot in the magazine. Your commentary on good works and intercession was super. I'm absolutely in accord about our small acts being saving acts. "Whatsoever ye do for the least of these ...," right?

Personal asides

Well, *I* didn't think you sounded critical of anyone — least of all toward an entire Order. (Cor. 13 — Love is not touchy, right?) Anything in your interview that sounded editorial seemed to flow from direct experience. Your remarks reminded me of another author, Augustine Baker who said, "the active livers" in and around monasteries frustrate the life of contemplatives by destroying their life of prayer. By "active livers" Baker did *not* mean people with active *minds*. He meant the busy-busy-busy Marthas of our world. I particularly admired your first paragraph in the interviewer's text where you say you've accepted that your active mind is, in part, an integral facet of your contemplation. Precisely so. Bravo to you. Good stuff.

Early morning prayers

Your early morning meditation reminds me a *bit* of my early a.m. ritual. This morning, for instance, I woke at 5. Here's my routine: I meditate for a while. Pray for a while (and/or sit in blessed stillness for God only knows how long), then read scripture for a while. Lately, I'm given to what I *think* is referred to as ejaculatory prayer. (What exactly is that? Maybe I'm mistaken.) Or I read scripture aloud: About 30 minutes on busy days and two to four hours on a relaxed day or Sunday. (My longest contemplative stint is mostly an interior movement that somehow infuses the entire day with prayer.) I take no credit. It's rooted in grace and sponsored, I suspect, by the prayer-of-the-heart (hesychast?).*

---

* Note to the reader: this theme crops up previously, see July 1996 letters. For more on that, see *The Way of the Pilgrim*, R. M. French, editor, New York: Seabury, 1965.

October

I salute your relaxed frame of mind, too. In his *Spiritual Direction*, Merton reminds us that spiritually advanced hearts just take things as they come. The lesser spiritual writers offer us specific formulas, lots of rules: Like, ten minutes of this and thirty of that, then five of this other. They "practice" forgiveness, with a big struggle — as if passing a kidney stone. If we love the rule book, we puff up with pride when we earn an A+ in prayer. (Loved your, "I don't pin myself down to any special way of praying ... I'm beginning to accept that that's O.K., that's how it is.") Praying is oneness with God, as natural as breathing and being breathed. Rewording the Zen saying, "God prays me."

"God prays me"

By the by, I am reviewing *Showings*. Did I mention? A national magazine might be interested. Would you prefer to write the review? I ask because they're expecting something, and if it will give you or your monastery or St. Clare some wanted visibility, I'm glad to pass the honors your way. (After all, you did mention that rendition of Julian's Revelations to me.) I'll keep on fine-tuning my review as I want to show it to Paulist before sending it on. There's time. Let me know.

Personal asides

Thank you also for encouraging me in terms of what you sense about my experience. Yes, I do feel God's leading — an increasingly palpable press to move toward a strictly contemplative life. I've decided next year to cut back my commercial writing and take two months off completely by myself, just to write and meditate.

On God's leadings

I was quite wrong to initiate the hermitage project as a non-profit and move it in a legalistic direction. That wore me out. Instead of simply listening to, and reflecting, the movement of the Holy Spirit, I chose a corporate process. Now I realize it's unfair to bring others along my route when they are not deeply empathic with it. How odd: My friends spot something in me they like, but when talk comes right down to the wire, they shy away from their own spiritual disclosures.

My pen-pal Father M reminded me over the phone that frequently one doesn't know the best way to go until taking one step, and then another, and then — after evaluating — correcting the next. Another friend calls this "no outlining." (Like you said, *stone by stone*.) Something in the title of that

Stone-by-Stone

81

A Spiritual Friendship

Cord article taps me on the shoulder. *And* your postscript on preparing for battle is timely: Didn't Saint Columbia rejoice, "Dear cell in which I have spent such happy hours, with the wind whistling through the loose stones and the sea spray hanging on my hair!" Precisely: The littlest happenings mirror our joy and awaken our energies.

On the wholeness of saints

You know, rarely do we read that a gentle person can be strong and effective, too. What I love about Julian (and also about St. Clare) is the absence of either obvious ultra-feminine or ultra-masculine tendencies: Wholeness shines through. They are at-one with the Mother-Father God. It strikes me as discounting to polarize well-integrated men and women into dualistic categories: Strong/weak/old/young.

I so appreciated the writer of that *Cord* article for acknowledging the true face of Clare as one of transcendence and light. That reflective light is our own true face. Aren't the saints sacred archetypes of our universal face, regardless of gender or creed?

Hey! Gotta go. Don't hold me up.

With thanks for your dear friendship, and may we show our true face each day.

H.

October

Sunday *
(Transcribed Tape)

Shalom, H.

It's just before morning prayer, and I'm walking out in the yard. Here's time for a tape. Right in front of me are two rabbits. I love rabbits. Of course we have groundhogs, too, on our four and a half acres here between the walls. It's a beautiful yard, but we don't have your woods. I've saved that picture you sent of the redwood grove surrounding your home and keep it (in the Sulivan book you gave me) to look at frequently. The forest is so peaceful.

Thank you for your letter. I'm glad that you listen to these tapes while driving around. It's easier for me to say what I've in mind on a tape. I'm learning to use the computer: Time consuming but fun, like a toy that's very interesting.

Yes, I was away and found it tiring. The Abbess let me go to Ohio to see my brother. In 1978 he had a terrible farm accident — he was run over by the back wheel of a tractor and wasn't expected to live. He's in good condition now and walks but can't travel here to see me. My sister, also a nun, and my cousin (who used to be a nun, left and got married and now has three sons) come down, too. We three have so much in common.

Personal asides

My brother started making redwood bird houses as a hobby. Now he can't hang onto them. People buy all he makes, and he sells them for around sixteen dollars each. His backyard is large, near a woods, and further down there's a lake that only the neighbors use. When the others go fishing, I like to sit and read.

You say that my relationship with my mother sounds enviable. Yes, we *were* on the same wavelength, but she died when she was 47. I had already entered the convent (at 18), so I didn't have much time with her. The time I did have taught me that a mother's love is special. Of course her love embraced my brother and sister in that same way. When my mother died, at her funeral I said to the others that I was special to

On family bonds

---

* Undated and out of sequence.

Mom. Then my sister said, "But *I* was." Then my brother said, "I thought *I* was." She had that kind of relationship with each one of us. My father was that way, too. More distant, but we knew we were loved. We grew up as lower middle-income people, yet very happy in our surroundings. My grandmother was the kind of person I could sit and talk to for hours.

Today when I go home, it seems some of us have little in common. At a recent family reunion, I felt like a stranger. This was my first family reunion. They used to hold it every year; now it's every other year. Anyway, traveling away from here makes me realize what I have, and that in a deeper way, this is my family now.

"Walking on eggs"

I particularly liked your comment that what may be loving and kind to *you* is often unloving and unkind to others. I relate to that. With certain relatives, we all must watch ourselves. Even those on the outskirts of each family notice the need to "walk on eggs." Every family faces this. The world is messy, and our lives are messy, and our own hearts are messy. But still we try. Still we reach out, in love.

You wrote that your happiest days came when you finally extricated yourself from the sway of family influence. That rings true for me. In a sense I did that but now long for family ties, because blood runs thicker than water, right? No matter how close we are to one another in this community, the others are not blood relatives. On the other hand, as I said, I'm more convinced than ever that I belong here, and that this is what I want out of my life. People like you, with whom I can share that fulfillment, know what I'm talking about.

On honoring father and mother

As for that "Honor Mother and Father" rule, my mother used to say that no matter how terrible parents may be, there's always a loyalty that you owe to your mother and father. As psychology, I don't know if that's solid advice, but she meant we must stand up for our family, against others who may laugh at them or criticize.

I, too, know how liberating it is to be able to say, "This is how it was in our family." My mother was ill half of my growing up years — since I was five. Not sick in bed, though. She

October

used to drag herself around. Only in later years did I realize how sick she really was, how self-sacrificing. When I was preparing to enter the convent, I told her, "I'd enter the convent and be a Sister, but since you're so ill, I can't leave you." (A part of me didn't want to enter the convent.) She answered, "Don't use that as your excuse. I want you to live your life fully." That was the truth. When I made first vows, my mother said, "Now I am ready to die." I made my vows that year; within the following year she died. I never knew how sick she was. Mom should have taken better care of herself. But she loved us and gave everything to us. She would tell us, "There's no love like a mother's love, no matter how bad the mother may be . . ." Yet it must be awfully hard to love a mother who is cruel.

I know what you mean: Looking at any experience through love's perspective (even our tough times in childhood), forgiveness becomes natural — our natural reconciliation, and indeed all the divisive elements of man-made creeds can be settled in eternity. At our family reunion for example, someone came up to me and announced she was marrying a Baptist and that she'd become a Baptist. Then flippantly she added, "Sorry." What could I say? Fortunately, someone else joined us and the tension dissipated. So that is a man-made creed or division that eternity and Love shall reconcile.

Love's perspective

To comment briefly on your childhood experiences of mystical union: That sort of experience seems very, very real. Looking back, I will share what I've shared with few others: When I made my first Holy Communion, I got up out of the pew, saying that all I wanted was Jesus, that all I wanted was to be a saint and holy. I laugh at that now, but it was a profound knowing — I remember the moment clearly — my veil, my white dress, that strong desire for holiness. Perhaps the nuns instilled that in me, too. Once, when I was in the sixth grade, I dreamed we'd been practicing how to answer the telephone in school. In my dream, the telephone rang. I answered it, saying, "This is the such-and-such residence. Who's calling, please?" And the answer I heard was, "Jesus." That stayed with me. To this day. Somehow young minds are

Mystical union in childhood

ready to receive these mystical experiences, and these profoundly touch them, stay with them the rest of their lives. We are each called back to that.

I'm enjoying *Morning Light* by Jean Sulivan with its lovely insights. One that sticks in mind is Sulivan's notion that we tend to read Jesus' parables as if they were legends — we don't apply them to ourselves, even though Jesus told those parables so that we'd take them to heart — to our deepest heart — and *live* his teachings.

Your new book sounds good. It's important to put on paper what's in our heart. I once read that a true writer must write to know what's within and, in the long run, that writing frees both the author and readers.

Lots of peace and love.

MF.

November
MORE MARY THAN MARTHA

In one of his books, Thomas Merton takes issue with the tendency of some religious persons to make much out of their techniques of prayer. Instead, he suggests that true contemplatives are relaxed in their prayers: They possess a unique disposition for a way of life that supports an interior unfolding, in this case union with the mystery of God. That disposition is reflected variously. MF informs us that the contemplative in community surrenders her will "to the common will" to meet God, both in self and in others. H's letters suggest mystical interiority, a recollection that, as Merton describes, is more like the absorption of a child in play, possessing "not only an alert spirit but also deep interest and love and wonder." [38]

It is that complete giving-up and giving-over of oneself to the Transcendent that Jesus of Nazareth advised when admonishing Martha to correct her priorities. Martha made herself useful, but Mary chose right relationship to Christ.

As the Bible tells us, Mary (Martha's sister) was seated at Jesus' feet, attentive to his every word. Martha, somewhat of a fuss-pot, *was preoccupied by her hostess role and distracted by her preparations.*

Characteristic of those who strive to get every little thing "just right," she even whined to the Lord that Mary wasn't doing her share, but Jesus replied,

> *Martha, Martha, you are worried*
> *and bothered about so many things;*
> *but only a few things are necessary, really only one,*
> *for Mary has chosen the good part,*
> *which shall not be taken away from her.* [39]

Both friends seem much more Mary than Martha. Each in her own way, and according to her intuitive grasp of her vocation, shows us how she has "chosen the good part, which shall not be taken away from her."

November

November 5, 1996

Dear H,

Thank you for your letter and kind words. It was good to hear that the article did not offend and I hope my Sister will understand.

The *Cord* magazine is yours to keep. I copied the "Spiritual Mothering" for myself but have not had the opportunity to read it yet (soon I hope). November 18-21 I will be in retreat, here at the Monastery. It's my turn with five others. We have what we call "the Martha, Mary retreat." The Marthas are in retreat but do the necessary chores, and the Marys need not do any. Then the next time the roles change. It works out beautifully. We use to pay a priest to preach to us; now we just have what we call a private retreat with Father PW giving us a good homily at the Mass. Sisters read their own topics, listen to tapes and just enjoy.

The Martha-Mary retreats

I ordered the book *A Dwelling Place for Wisdom* from the library and resonate greatly with it. It is tremendous. Thank you for exposing me to this man, Panikkar. Some Poor Clare nuns, who were here to work on a committee for Clarian Theology, spoke of this Panikkar in the sense that he is *the* new theologian for the 21st century. Thank you. I am taking notes on his book. He is deep and at times one has to re-read what he says. Wonderful "stuff."

A theologian for the 21st century

As for Augustine Baker and his term "the active livers," I like that. Baker wrote a book *Contemplative Prayer* from Sancta Sophia (Holy Wisdom). Interesting that you should quote him. He lived in the 16th century and we have a copy of his book published in 1906 which I read 10 or so years ago. Hmmm.

I love your relaxed morning — very contemplative. Here I get involved with the Mass and other tasks, but I always remember all is prayer.

Morning prayers; ejaculatory prayer

My relaxed frame of mind you salute. I do a lot of bending because I have learned to do so. However, one gives up one's personal will for something better. So I bend. That is why I read so much of the concentration camp books to see how they survived and learned from them. Yes, living life to

A Spiritual Friendship

the full is prayer. Like the story of the Rabbi who said that when he dies God will ask, "Did you enjoy my earth? Were you truly yourself and not trying to be Abraham?" Prayer helps us be who we are — to the hilt. Love those tid-bits.

As to ejaculatory prayer: It is either oral or just said with the mind, like *"O Lord, you are all that I have in the land of the living,"* which for some reason I have made mine. It acts as what some might call a mantra.

Personal asides

Now, here's a story. We had a handy man (R) who worked with our custodian B — about whom I've told you. R was an Episcopalian who, when he worked in our chapel, would always stop and kneel before the tabernacle where we house the Blessed Sacrament-White Host that we believe is the Real Presence of Jesus. One day I was with R and I quickly passed the Tabernacle without making a reverent bow or kneel, and R scolded me: "And you are a Catholic." Now ever since then, when I pass the Tabernacle, I bow and say the quote above. R has since died, and I have that connection with him and the Lord.

Confession time: I must confess that I never completely read *Showings*, only parts, but I just could never finish it no matter how many times I tried. If I cannot find a book grabbing me, I set it aside. So I could not possibly review the book but thank you for the offer. That was thoughtful of you.

Enclosed, a nice handy translation of the New Testament (approved by bishops for children, but perfect for me) with Psalms and Proverbs. I have a copy which I carry with me in my pocket.

Must go.
Love and peace in Christ,

MF.

November

November 7, 1996

Dear MF:

Did I ever answer your letter about the critique you felt you'd given of another Order in that fine interview? (Seems like I did, then perhaps you sent another round of interview texts to me.) Anyway, as I believe I said, you didn't sound critical at all — not in any way. Not even slightly. Some people are just unbelievably touchy. You must be well-known too, like the others interviewed. Being so naturally modest, you probably don't even realize that.

Now it's my turn to enclose an interview I was recently criticized for — so much, that the periodical's publisher nearly didn't print the piece. Apparently, my response — to some question that the interviewer added *after* the interview had been completed — caused the entire editorial staff to spend a whole day arguing both sides of the point. They didn't like my statement that our vocational summons is to Christ — *that's* our call — and, even if it means stepping into the unknown, we are obliged to follow. (Mind you, this is a Christian periodical.) The editor phoned to see if I'd modify my point of view. Fat chance, says I. (But politely.)

Paradox of spiritual growth

The more vividly I experience (and respond to) the grace of the Holy Spirit and try to honor Its leadings in everyday affairs, the more hidden I want to be. At the same time, the more outspoken I seem on behalf of that precise experience. (Just like with the controversial interview: Hiddenness and outspokenness hardly dovetail. Right? A strange paradox.)

Well, I've bitten into a rather bitter apple in deciding to relocate from my serene forest home next year, to set up that hermitage in Washington State. It may not be a right choice, so I'll stay flexible. I've chosen a small bustling town with a fine airport, university and excellent support services. I'll occupy a minuscule — really *tiny* — cottage, remodel it and then evaluate whether it's appropriate. There's room to fix up a lovely, small garden. I have no clue how to proceed and feel vulnerable in leaving my secure nest. More sailing off toward the Utter East. Along the lines that Father M proposed, I'll

Personal asides

A Spiritual Friendship

take one step, then two, then evaluate, then correct myself: An intuitive unfolding.

Developing faith through trials

Alas, the autobiography I've worked on for the last *year* (and feel is so grand) was roundly rejected for being uncommercial. Back to square one. I *think* I know how to fix it but am not yet sure I want to. What with the hermitage, it's hard to focus on this now. How one manages without faith, I'll never know. It seems as if faith develops *through* challenges — by our "not fainting" for example — and then, mysteriously, unfolds our good in concrete solutions. Our good is the good that God is, no?

I do love Julian for saying how "our good Lord answered" her own doubts:

> *I can make all things well,*
> *and I shall make all things well,*
> *and I will make all things well;*
> *and You will see yourself that every kind of thing*
> *will be well ...*[40]

I reassure you that your interview sounded mild and peaceful and totally accepting of others.

May we all rest sweetly in God's Peace.

In His Name,

H.

On spiritual growth and friends

P.S. Do you remember our conversation earlier in the year about spiritual growth and friends? A wonderful insight from Murray who writes of the person at Bethesda who asks Jesus for healing. First, Jesus asks, "Wilt thou be made whole?" Murray says this is *our* question, too. Our answer must be an unequivocal "Yes," coupled with faith that Christ *can* heal: Some are unwilling to "entirely forsake their walk in the world ... The walk *in* Christ and *like* Christ is too straight and hard; they will not do it." Then he tells us to stop looking to any other *person* for assistance:

November

... Christ wants us to look up to Him as our only Helper. "I have no man to put me in" must be our cry. Here on earth there is no help for me ..."[41]

In other words, our surrender to the Spirit within exposes spiritual growth, a yielding that has nothing to do with others.

A Spiritual Friendship

November 26, 1996

Dear MF,

What a sweet surprise at the post office. Thanks so much for the lovely New Testament. It was dear of you to think of me.

"From death to Life"   I certainly do understand your remark about Cardinal Bernadin passing "from death to Life." That expresses my sensibilities precisely. In our foolishness we squash everything divinely unbounded into some finite box. One day we'll realize that, in God, life is good *forever*. Your dream about Bernadin was inspiring, even prophetic. I loved your remarking how well he looked. (I trust your friend who knew him is of a mind and heart to understand your dream and will not grieve his passing on too sorely.)

Personal asides   Well, this will be a longish letter. After the New Year I'll be very busy, unable to write much for a few months. My hermitage project moves along nicely now that I've unloaded the bureaucratic element.

I plan to spend each Winter here at this little woods-home. Even so, leaving is not automatic. Yet more lessening of human attachment as "the Son has nowhere to lay his head." One grows to feel at home anywhere. Right?

Do you have access to the Internet?

On spiritual persistence   More publishers' rejections. First round of New York publishers' opinions: They want me to make it a how-to book. In a pig's eye. My agent is shocked. She loves its essay feel, says it's rich stuff. (She has not liked some other works of mine, so I trust her word.) Plus, I like it myself. Anyway, each day I remind myself that I am working for God's glory and not for man. This month both your letter (and Brother H's) reminder to have courage helps. (Courage: To persist *despite* fear or rejection.) Courage — and persistence — are spiritual qualities that unfold the truth. In Browning's words, "Truth is within ourselves and takes no rise from outward things."

Less personal sense   To endure in trust, simple-mindedly, when disappointments come is to live the truth that all works together for the good. Whenever I forget my "personal sense" as another friend calls

November

it, the yoke is light. Don't you think we do ourselves a great disservice by overanalyzing *why* a thing didn't work out as we pre-envisioned, or why (psychologically speaking) we're motivated in this or that direction? I've actually rejected most of what I was taught about psychology in graduate school. It is, pardon me, a crock.

Most psychologists are full of "small self." (Translation: Full of personal egoism and illusion.) Do you know what I mean? Self-analysis invites the small, false-self to subtly engulf us in doubt, alarm or fear that we need this or that thing to be complete. Grounding ourselves in God's Word, we *are* complete. Perfectly empty, we are a living trust.

Self-emptying and completeness

Bernard of Clairvaux wrote that the remedy for all wounds — the help we need, the correction for our faults, the source of progress — is found when we pray perfectly for "there is no reason to ask the Word for anything other than himself since he *is all things*." [42] Lovely reasoning, no? Here again, the true saint lifts our thought directly to God, lets us think God's thoughts, know ourselves as we are known — like deJaegher who asks, "*Am I not the thought of God, the fruit of His thought?*"

By the way, *my* confession to *you* is that I don't read Julian of Norwich (or Sulivan) straight through, either, but I never let that stop me from writing a review. Merton and Panikkar and a few others — now that's another story.

I enjoyed a most refreshing Thanksgiving. Today (Friday), I am reviewing certain letters stuffed away in files. Deeply moving. Some of yours were included in those stacks. I revisited your tapes. In weeks to come, I'll respond to some overlooked aspects of those. A gentle kindness emanates from your voice and encourages me. I am grateful.

Personal asides

About such back-and-forth correspondences and spiritual friendships, I've mentioned that it seems as we move toward real emptiness, we are naturally (or supernaturally?) *dis*inclined to cling to anyone else through special friendships (e.g., like the family, the "best friend," the lover, the mentor or authority figure). God is our source of renewal. Our whole being leans into God Who is closer than our breath. Spiritual friendships uniquely release us to that reorientation.

On spiritual friendship

95

A Spiritual Friendship

Mysteriously, the other's *own* union with God intervenes on our behalf as a prayerful movement to establish us, as Ruysbroeck puts it, in "fruitive love" — i.e., we are *with* God, without intermediary and become one spirit *with* God. ("Abide in Me.") Spiritual friendships encourage us toward our Perfect Friend. Having been wrought in Christ, no other attachment is possible. In that sense, even the mother-child bond — as your own mother proved — puts the spiritual life of self-and-other above traditional, relational "forms." At the same time real compassion, the heart's love, grows vivid. This is why Mother Teresa functioned as she did in India's grimy back streets with what appeared supernatural energy.

To one of your taped remarks: Yes, blood is thicker than water, *but* the Blood of the Lamb is thickest of all. No?

Spiritual friends as mentors

A spiritual friendship imparts the mentor's spirit.[43] I identify with Bernard of Clairvaux because he, too, had a worldly side. He was an artist, a busy Abbott and a monk and spent much time away from his monastery. Anyway, he says so crisply (I'm sorry to paraphrase) that our conversion returns us to the Father *through* the Son *in* the Spirit, while all that is human about us remains in Jesus and is simultaneously transformed in glory (Bernard says "trans-situated") into the very life of God. Isn't that beautiful? Bernard insists that humility, fraternal compassion and prayer lead us from meditating on our lesser truths (he uses the word "wretched" and I'd use "personal sense") to the contemplation of God's truth — pure love — and to God's mercy which has been revealed in Christ. (Of course, Clairvaux was speaking about and for cloistered monks, but he addresses me, too, as if he were right here.)

My point is that a genuine spiritual progression lessens human attachments on "special" friends while letting us attend to others in ways fashioned by God's love. Ah ... Sorry to ramble.

All peace to you and everyone at the Monastery. H.

P.S. Your Panikkar quotes were super. With great thanks. What about Ewert Cousins? He's a little academic for my taste, but Brother H sent me a tape of Ewert that inspired me totally.

December
VITAL DAILY LIFE

*W*E HAVE TRIED TO EXPLAIN *how the contemplative life, and particularly its prayer is "of the heart," is a life reflecting the Love that is God. The life itself enlivens love, faith and a divine focus. It also promotes a certain independence, firmness of intent and spiritedness. This is true not simply of the formally religious, but of solitary, well-focused artists as well. Georgia O'Keefe, an American master, lived an increasingly monastic existence from mid-life through her death in her 90s.*

Quite consciously, O'Keefe distanced herself from her peers, refusing to socialize with the busy subculture of artists living nearby. She preferred her own company and her primary love — painting. She identified so fully with her work that once, while preparing for a showing, when someone criticized her for being fussy in hanging her art, she replied, in effect, "You'd be meticulous too if you were hanging yourself on the wall."

December's letters illustrate something of that same spirited self-understanding: H refuses to sell her new book if it means commercializing her voice; MF recounts how she entered her contemplative order without her family's understanding.

A Spiritual Friendship

On a celebratory note, we learn that the daily routines of cloistered life are altered during the winter holidays, much as are our own schedules, and MF's remarks show us that nuns and monks may differ in their use of evening hours.

⑥

December

December 15, 1996

Dear H,

Thank you for your last letter, and I am glad you like the portable New Testament. It also has Psalms and Proverbs. I know that the Psalms are among your favorite texts, and I personally like this translation. The Psalms are my favorite, too. Many of the saints, among them Francis, said we should always carry the Gospels close to our heart. Well, I carry it in a side pocket.

A friend and Sister who knew Bernadin, called me to tell me that she had the opportunity to attend the funeral. She said she felt that the Cardinal was still looking out for her. *Personal asides*

He, like other holy ones, seemed to take his death in worshipful, graceful stride. St. Clare, as she lay dying, prayed, *"Thank you, my God, for having created me."* St. Francis, when he was dying, was carried through the local towns and villages on the way to his final resting place but asked to stop that he might say one final prayer for his beloved town of Assisi: *On Worshipful deaths*

> *May God bless you, holy town, so that many souls are saved by you. May many servants of God dwell in you, and may many of your inhabitants be chosen to enter the kingdom of eternal life.*

It pleases me to hear that your hermitage moves at its right pace. Somewhere in the Gospels the Jewish Rabbi Gamaliel (Acts 5:35) says that if the Jesus movement is of God, nothing can stop it and if not, it will fall apart. My loose translation. I feel that way with our building project and you seem to feel that with your own.

No, we do not have access to the Internet but probably that will come. Don't feel too badly about the rejections of your book. Merton faced many rejections. Still, I know it is hard to take rejection on any level. William Johnston SJ says that the greatest tool in one's spiritual life is rejection. *Rejection: tool of spiritual growth*

Right now I am reading *As Sure As the Dawn* by Patrick J. Howell SJ, a Jesuit who recovered from a breakdown and now guides others to healing. It has some good spots. One passage brought tears to my eyes: A story of a young man who wasn't sure how to cope with the losses in his life. One day he looked up at the blue sky and said, "Thank you," and felt something just sweep through him. Anyway, as the author tells it is most moving.

On leaps of faith

Yes, we must constantly have faith that when we take the spiritual leap, the net will be there. If we are striving to do God's will, God will bless our effort. That I am sure of. And if one asks, "How do we know it is God's will?" I say it is God's will that we reach out to Him in any manner. You are. As you say: Faith leads you to God.

Perils of over-analysis

Loved your reference to over-analyzing. I do that so much and your friend is right: To forget the "personal sense" and move along in faith with our faces toward the stars, like flint (that image from Scripture), that is a solid thought. Thank you.

Selected readings

I am reading Sulivan little by little, but he is not as good as Sinetar or Panikkar. *The Cloud of Unknowing* I have tried many times but never finish. As to the ennigram stuff: I like some of it, just to help me to know myself but do not read books about it because it is too much head tripping, as you once said. I have not read Ewert Cousins, but an article by him in *America* magazine, (a Jesuit magazine, which I love) was very, very good. He is heavy though, I agree.

Personal asides

Yesterday we had seven candidates for the priesthood here for Mass and dinner. They are hoping to be Franciscans so are exploring our part of the Charism. At dinner I sat with Friar A, a lawyer, and someone else whose name escapes me. One of the things the lawyer said is how hard the initial training is — it seems to throw one back into childhood.

As our life is very intense, so our usual table talk is light, but I always enjoy exchanges and dialogue.

I enjoyed your interview in that religious magazine. The Q and A was lively, and I'll respond to it later. I am so glad you share those things with me, for I like to share my ideas and articles with you. We are all different and some of the issues I want to discuss, Sister M and you share with me. Christmas

December

blessings and my love. Thank you for YOU and blessings on all your endeavors, especially your new hermitage.

Love,

MF.

P.S. *Monastic Interreligious Dialogue* for Fall was excellent. You sent me that subscription, but do you receive the magazine yourself? (Just realized Ewert Cousins is written up in there, not *America* magazine.)

A Spiritual Friendship

December 29, 1996

Dear H,

Peace and every blessing for the New Year. I was going to make a tape, but I did not get a chance to ask the mail carrier about how to send them since they have been coming back ripped apart, etc. So the computer is the next choice.

Festive holiday schedule

We have been goofing off since Christmas:

1. Christmas eve Mass 10:00 p.m.,

2. Christmas day late dinner with dessert in the evening about 6:00 and unwrapping of gifts,

3. December 26: Those who are thinking of entering gave us a party,

4. December 27: The Knights of Columbus from St. Mary's cooked, served and washed the dishes for us,

5. December 28: Sister M and I had a Bingo party for the Sisters,

6. Today, December 29: The Feast of the Monastery, dedicated to the Holy Family so we are having a special meal and later dessert,

7. Tomorrow we are having company, some lay folks who want to visit the Sisters,

8. December 31: A quiet day, in preparation for the New Year,

9. D and I are having a party in the evening with ice cream and a video, *Roommates*, with Peter Falk. I hope it is good, and I hope it is clean (that is in language and situations).

So after that we should get back to normal. Whatever that is. I do hope you had a good Christmas.

Thank you for your last letter of December 19th. With all you have to do, you are taking time to work on a gift for me? Just your letters make me happy, and I know that you have to

December

take time for them from something else. So they are greatly appreciated.

    I think I would have liked your friend G. But elitist? You? I think not, since you are hanging out with me. However, for whatever reason I may choose friends who think of themselves as elitists. Father PC (my friend who might call himself elitist) can't be bothered with those who talk about the weather. He said there are three kinds of people: ones who discuss things; those who discuss people; and those who discuss ideas. G seems like a lovely person with whom I would have liked to exchange ideas and share funny stories. I love dry wit. My sister has that quality. My humor borders on corny, but I do love a hearty sense of humor. Just to show you how I am, I received a gift of a sweater for Christmas and wore it today to morning prayer with the label tag still hanging on under the arm. That reminds me of the movie, *New Leaf*, where the heroine did that, too. Anyway, it gave some of us a good laugh. *Personal asides*

    Yes, we know when our friends accept, respect and admire us. We feel safe in their presence as they allow us to be who we are, with all our faults and foibles. That is probably why G liked you — you accepted him as is: No airs, no demands, no "nuttin'" — just sheer acceptance. What a gift to another human being! *On the mutual regard of friends*

    Well, about the use of evening hours: After using all the day's energy on research, writing or reading, one must relax or just be entertained. I understand that. After praying and reading and working, in the evening all I like to do is read the comics, watch the news or skim books lightly and flop into bed — maybe play *one* game of solitaire on the computer to sharpen my wits. Once in a while I watch a video with the Sisters — a comedy or mystery (if not too scary). Usually around the holidays we get together for a video. (The Trappists may go to the back of their barn, smoke cigars and play pinochle. We watch a video.) *On use of evening hours*

    The new Sisters are still discerning their decision (i.e., praying about it). We will see. Time will tell where wisdom lies. As with all those religious of old who ran off and entered *Discernment in cloistered life* a cloister, they found that life difficult. One cannot run away from oneself: You bring yourself with you. If you do not have things squared away in your life, the old baggage from your family of origins spills out and into community which causes havoc to others.

Yes, I like DeSales's spirituality. He is very down to earth.

Encouragement & spiritual direction

When I decided to enter contemplative, cloistered life, even my own sister — a Sister of Charity who teaches in a Catholic school — did not understand why I did it or what I thought I was going to gain. Most of my Catholic friends did not approve, but a Hindu friend from India understood and supported my choice. So be encouraged by your former spiritual director, Sister M.R. Many are called to the contemplative life, but people turn their backs and do not want to go. However, once you venture out and set sail, there is no turning back. You will no longer be happy with the old way. You are sailing into deeper waters and beautiful spaces.

Hey, gotta go. Don't hold me up.

Next time, a tape.

Thank you, too, for YOU,

Shalom and love, MF.

December

Letter Excerpt December 31, 1996

Dear MF,

The wind chimes are clanging (the wind is hooping it up in the trees). Mesmeric sounds. I love it. I'm tucked away snugly at home. The power's been out for two days.

I made a delicious lunch over a tiny Bunsen burner — hot veggie soup, a broiled hot dog (skewered and cooked over the lone flame) and piping hot Earl Grey tea. Nibbled all day on Christmas goodies — especially fudge from the Gethsemani Abbey. Divine. My house is dark during the winter, even during daylight. At dusk I light plumbers' candles: Stubby, fantastic things that seemingly last forever. They only cost 65¢ each — the greatest thing since sliced bread (in a storm, anyway). And if need be, I have my pot bellied stove. Today is warmish, so I won't use it. The sun is pink-rose in the winter's haze. (Thoreau, eat your heart out.)

Rural, winter life

On your several tapes from way back: First, congratulations on what seems a year of accomplishment — Your interview was published, you met and had your picture taken with the Holy Father (which I never properly acknowledged), and you've served on numerous educational and interfaith committees. Quite a year, don't you think? Considering you lead a cloistered life. I assess the end of each year, so forgive me if I apply that habit to you.

Yearly assessments

Several times now I've wanted to say that when I read about the small irritations of cloistered living, I'm reminded of normal family and business life. One always watches one's words — how one says every minuscule thing — and forever restrains the natural tendency to boast, over-talk or betray confidences. This is not all bad. But sometimes the most diplomatic corporate types are a touch *too* slick. They're the artful dodgers who finesse and manipulate and would do well to practice Scripture's "Let your yea be yea, and your nay, nay."

Corporate vs. cloistered diplomacy

It's easier for me to control my natural enthusiasm since living this simple life, but still not automatic. When I'm with others, that new restraint translates into strengthened self-control — as if at the ground of being I'm bolstered. Good

> *The kiss of death to innocence*

old Tauler writes that if we would be transformed into God then we must free ourselves of our nature, our inclinations, our self-opinion. Self-opinion, yes, but God gave us our nature, no? Tauler's is a sure-fire method to draw a perfectionistic attention to *oneself*. Here again, he's so keen on *self-effort*. I prefer the notion of keeping our *eyes* on God, for aren't we ultimately infused with the attributes of the One we love? (The more virtuous we are in our own eyes or by external measures, the more full of self. Isn't grace unmerited favor?) Let's not chase *human* perfection.

Or maybe I say that because I find myself unable to do all that Tauler instructs. Anyway, God made me and knows me, and I trust He'll work it out so that I am purified by the life he's given me to lead. If I can just be true to who I am — namely a God-centered "innocent" for whom God is *immediately present* in a wholly intimate and completely available sense — isn't that sufficient? Not self-perfection counts, but trusting that God is perfect Love, right?

> *Trust God, not self-effort*

I love what Murray says: To the prayerful (not necessarily to the blemish-free) the Holy Spirit gives authority to do divine work and use Christ's name and abide in the anointing; to the prayerful the Holy Spirit comes to live as Truth, uniting them to God.[44] Isn't that oneness the harmonizing element between all believers, no matter their doctrine, no matter how seemingly "imperfect" they are?

There seems a vast divide between those — like Julian of Norwich or Merton — who commune with God in that intimate way and those who obtain their religious fulfillments through some organized or legitimized methods. After working this out on paper, I see that, even here, if love resides in either, God has His hand on both.

So much for pontificating. I only meant to say "Happy New Year" and congratulate you on a good year gone by.

Peace and all blessings,

H.

January
SUMMING UP

$\mathcal{E}_{VEN}$ A BRIEF REVIEW of these collected letters shines light on the attributes shared by spiritual friends, namely

> *keen and clearly stated ardor for God,*

> *mutual respect and support for one another's deepening devotional life,*

> *expressed (not merely felt) appreciation for the distinctive worshipful relationship each has with God,*

> *a high degree of trust and openness (one gets the feeling that everything shared is grist for their spiritual mill),*

> *a love of people, specifically and universally, enhanced by good humor and an even temper.*

When disappointed or frustrated, neither fusses against others or rails against life. Quite spontaneously, each reconciles whatever is happening in the peace that passes understanding. Thus a spiritual

A Spiritual Friendship

friendship also underscores the wisdom of associating with those who are gentle and harmonious, as it is written:

> Make no friendships with an angry man;
> and with a furious man thou shalt not go,
> lest thou learn his ways and get a snare to thy soul. [45]

The January missives seem to summarize the year's themes: Repeating the value of optimism and faith during trials; the power of God's ideas, the importance of encouragement to spiritual life; the virtue of trust and the wish to release all things to God.

The two continue describing the particulars of their daily life during the holidays. Again, we note the intrinsic lightness of a reflective life. Sister MF sheds light on her contemplative studies when describing a Scripture-sharing session. Sister MF, we learn, also puts pictures in her devotional books. Her practice is reminiscent of early monks who, according to Professor Lawrence Cunningham, memorized the Psalms and sang them in the cloister and entered the world of the Psalmist, "an other who has had profound experiences of God with which one frequently resonates." [46] The focus on a familiar devotional text extends the prayer life, as Cunningham muses,

> There is something wonderful about a beaten-up, heavily marked, tattered Bible. Madeline Delbrel, the French Catholic activist who lived a little more than a year ago, stuffed her Bible with snapshots, clippings, ticket stubs, postcards and other detritus to remind her that she was praying in the world of people and events. She called these scraps "icons of humanity" that prompted one to celebrate the liturgy of life."[47]

The tone of H's letters informs us again of what Underhill calls the mystic temperament — in particular "that tending forward" into transfiguring love that carries one over created things in end-

January

less, absorbed contemplation of the Infinite and "made one with Truth." [48]

Moreover, this month we better appreciate each friend's basic simplicity of heart as evidenced by Sister MF's description of the "holiness of jelly beans" and H's picnic in the woods with bearded workmen.

So do the friends reveal their inner child of innocence and "of such is the Kingdom of Heaven."

A Spiritual Friendship

January 1, 1997

Dear MF,

It's storming fiercely. Rain has been coming down in buckets for days. Even so, Christmas was shining. I trust yours was wonderful as well. Mine was spent at home, cozily, and with great good friends (with R and S and others). Seems everyone considered what I'd want (instead of the old fruitcake routine).

Personal asides

There's nothing I *really* want or need, but I do collect old English teapots and this year received some complements to that: Some Spode and gorgeous cut crystal and so on. One day all of this will go to the hermitage to be enjoyed by its visitors. Receiving anything these days, I envision it warming up others with beauty or — as with the books — with the wisdom that edifies me. The idea makes me inordinately glad. (Each is to be a good steward in her own way, yes?)

Favorite books

Speaking of books, I ordered the entire Paulist series of *Ancient Christian Writers* including St. Augustine's Sermons and St. Gregory the Great, *Notes on Pastoral Care*; and St. John Chrysostom's *Instructions on Baptism*. Nearly all high-caliber hardbacks. Thrilling. There's even an old volume of St. Augustine's on the literal meaning of Genesis (this in reference to your so enjoying the PBS series). That grand dame of sculpture, Louise Nevelson, reputedly said the only reality she recognized is *her* reality, apprehended through her work. I feel like that, in writing and in collecting these classic books. Neat, no?

Well, it is a great, good honor to be quoted in your Calendar of Quotes for the new year. Thank you for that and for your recent letter. (Your computer skills, by the way, are improving swimmingly; each letter you send looks increasingly professional.)

What a shame your friend didn't believe your dream. I'm always refining the skill of discerning to whom I can say what and guarding my words so that I speak the unadulterated truth without either hurting or placating or making small talk. The holidays bring lots of help for that practice, don't you think?

January

Your St. Clare quote is absolutely lovely. Thank you for thinking to send it.

Now, as for publisher rejections: No, I truly don't mind (after the reflexive "Ouch" of disappointment, that is). Rejection at the start is almost a sure sign that better things will follow *if* one holds true to course. My original publisher turned down last year's offering, yet I sold it eventually to a larger, NY publisher — for much more money. It sold out completely in hardback and is still going strong in paperback. It's lack of faith that creates problems, no? Chambers writes that faith must be tested; it becomes a personal possession only through use.

On faith during rejection

Yesterday a best-selling author on CSPAN-TV described how, for one whole year, she tried in vain to sell her book proposal. *Every* major publisher rejected it. She wrote the piece anyway (as an article for her *college* magazine, no less). Only then did a first-rate NY publisher fully back her book. They gave her advances, publicity, editorial support — the works. Her book hit the best seller list and has been translated into 15 different languages. She said success gives her a new, full-time job: Traveling around the country lecturing about her triumph. She now longs to write. Her story edifies.

That publishing scenario underscores our various exchanges about faith, as well as your recent Rabbi Gamaliel quote: *If something is God's idea, nothing can stop it.* In terms of such spiritual victory, St. Teresa of Avila grew weary when reading authors who presented our perfection as a goal obstructed by "a thousand obstacles."

Nothing can stop God's idea

She shut any book which tired her brain, preferring to read scripture like a child in God's arms.[49]

Here again, I love the Saints for so delicately pointing us toward divine union (and with such hopefulness). Were it not for them, who would not crumble from want of spiritual companions with whom to explore such ideas as completion? How I love (and re-read) my old, worn out book on trust by Paul deJaegher. Years ago I sent you some thoughts from PDJ admonishing us never to say holiness is not for us, never to feel we are too unworthy for completion or that it is too late

On the optimism of true saints

111

to become a saint or even that we are at a standstill, spiritually. Rather he says we should ...

> *cherish with jealous solicitude this desire for holiness which in itself is a great grace that God imparts like a precious seed deep in our hearts, trust God to bring us unfailing to perfection's port.*[50]

God bless deJaegher and all the saints.

That storm wails away or whatever storms do — and anticipating a power-outage I must sign off to unplug all my computer/printer/lighting paraphernalia and cook up a bit of din-din before being reduced to candlelight. (One of my Christmas gifts was a spectacular cut-glass hurricane lamp. When one puts a lit candle in it, the flame-light dancing on the walls and ceiling is absolutely celestial.)

Oh, yes, almost forgot — Happy New Year.

More later,

H.

January

January 2, 1997

Greetings, MF:

In response to your December 29th missive, for which I heartily thank you: It was fun scanning your holiday schedule. What with the power being on and off (mostly off) for three days, here's a sample of my schedule for today:

Personal asides

1. Up at 7 a.m. (slept in today), relieved to find the power on,

2. Ventured out to get the mail (2 boxes *full*) and discovered several trees — bull pines, mostly — fallen over. Thankfully none touched my home, yard or driveway,

3. 10 a.m. — returned from post office and marketing with more storm supplies: batteries, "plumbers candles" (the fat, long-burning variety — Must-Haves out here),

4. 10:30 a.m. — inspected the property to see if any trees were tilting precipitously toward my house,

5. 10:50 a.m. — called the fallen-tree patrol (our local Good Guys from the homeowners' association) about three bull pines, leaning dangerously near my dear roof. I expected a lengthy delay, but a whole team of them popped right over,

6. 11:00 a.m. — a *squad* of Tree Guys drove over with hook and ladders and a tractor and trucks and dogs and buzz saws and a whole lot of beards. They agreed, right there on the spot, to take down *four huge pines*. I mean within about 5 minutes of my call, here they stood at the ready, yellow rain slickers and boots and all, at my front door. Impressive. (I don't think I know them, but they call me by first name. Am I known for getting fired up (or at least all prickly) if things aren't handled properly? This strikes my funny bone: In *my* mind, I'm quiet, mild mannered, so easy going. It always amazes me when I intimidate

113

A Spiritual Friendship

anyone (especially big, hairy Tree-Guys). Somehow I can see it: Little peppery women can be trouble.

I took snapshots of the tree-cutting process when B, the Primary Big-Tree Guy entrusted with the heinous buzz-saw, climbed up a tree. When developed, I'll send one. Those falling pines thunder down, and B is truly brave.

On human tenderness

The sweet thing about these seemingly rugged types is how tender they really are. I made coffee and such for us all, and upon setting it out, their comportment changed drastically: Rough and tumble workers became gentlemen with crooked-pinkies as the dainty sipping of hot beverage began. (A little picnic in the woods: Bone china cups amidst greasy black chain-saw blades and orange tractors. Truth, life and beauty coalesced in one instant.) You had to be there. One Bearded Woodsguy went berserk over my Black Bamboo and flowering vines. Another swooned over the brass wind chimes. Both accepted cuttings of the vines, and one promised to bring me some crimson holly in exchange.

Beauty heals

Have you ever met anyone who wasn't exquisitely affected by Beauty? So heartwrenchingly human. So divine. (Like you once said, one gets overwhelmed by the sheer goodness of others — kings, clowns and woodspeople alike.) What about piping Bach into our prisons and treating prisoners with respect and refinement and simply engulfing them in beauty? Now there's a concept.

Your use of evening hours sounds lovely. There's nothing remotely better than a good mystery (book or film) — one of the finest ways to spend time. (The *New Leaf* is one of my favorites, too. So cute.)

On the contemplative life

Your remark about contemplative life is so true. Wasn't it Merton who wrote that contemplatives do not take their prayer methods too seriously but do take God seriously and are famished for truth. That phrase *"famished for truth"* resonates with such honesty. The contemplative life which I actualize more singlemindedly each year is really "it": God's Beauty, Truth and Presence stirring in — as — my very soul. God bless Paul deJaegher for saying that such desire is, in

114

January

itself, "a great grace that God implants like a precious seed down in our hearts."

That sort of uplifting direction is precisely the gift Sister M.R. gave me and why I am so grateful to her — and to you — for encouraging me. If your Catholic friends (and even your own sister) didn't understand your deciding to live a cloistered life, you can imagine my uneasiness all these years when conversing with family and friends. Eventually one learns. However, such social tension is nothing — a mere trifle and purifying — and the least we can sustain for so great a richness as contemplative life affords. I feel so tremendously glad, so grateful, to enjoy this blessing and this Love, while still alive. Certainly you who speak of the beauty of nature and silence know what I mean.

On spiritual encouragement

Well, gotta go. Don't hold me up!

Happy New Year to you and Sister M and all my distant friends at the Monastery.

Love in Christ — to us all.

H.

P.S. In reference to what I'd been searching for, about Mary: I recently discovered Bernard of Clairvaux's line that "she became the mother of all the sons of God," the perfect realization and the embodiment of achieved sanctification, *and* we can have "unlimited confidence" in her. And in Martha Wilcox, an early 1900s metaphysician, this terrific thought: That Mary's mode of consciousness *was* Truth. She fulfilled the prophecy of Isaiah and knew there must be human evidence (or manifested proof) of the invisible, inexhaustible God that underlies all visible things ...

Mary's mode of thought as Truth

Well, *now* I really gotta go.

H.

A Spiritual Friendship

January 27, 1997
(Transcribed Tape)

Well, H,

I answer your last letter by taping this for you. It's Sunday, and I'm on a retreat or quiet day. We have to go to the Eucharistic celebration, Mass. Then we're free to pray and to eat by ourselves. I laughed when reading that you're continually eating. I am, too — today. I have a little bit of meat and rice, and then I made some popcorn, then got some nuts and an orange and some Hershey kisses. I'll save the Hershey kisses for tonight's supper and will eat the popcorn in between, and for dessert. And I'll probably nibble all that from now until suppertime. Like you, I prefer not to eat a whole lot at one sitting. On these quiet days, you can eat frequent, small meals because you're by yourself.

Personal asides

I'm glad you had a wonderful Christmas. Another thing, don't feel that you have to send any present. Your letters are gift enough for me, honestly. As you've sent such a nice, long letter and as we don't just talk "religious gab," there is real substance to your remarks. Feel no obligation to send me anything. I greatly enjoy your letters. They truly lift me up.

I didn't realize you collected old English teapots. That's nice. Your hermitage will have some lovely things. In a fantasy or in dreaming, I often think that if I was out in the secular world, I'd own a little book shop and serve coffee there — all different flavors — and invite lecturers to share their ideas about books, and I'd display teapots and beautiful coffee mugs, as you say, to warm people up with beauty. I like that notion.

Pictures in Bibles

There is so much to read, and I still haven't done as much as I should, but I read a little bit each day. As I said, I'm thoroughly into this new bible. I liked your storm pictures and the cutting of the big bull pine and put these on my new devotional bible — the one I got for Christmas.

When I began my calendar of quotes, each had to be quite short because the computer wouldn't accept longer ones. My computer actually got to the point where it wouldn't work, and Father J introduced me to a computer whiz, Mr. S, who once

January

worked for NASA. I really needed him to clean out the computer. He fixed it up, left the desktop things I use, and now it's just wonderful. That's where I got into difficulty with that calendars of quotes. I have many more of your quotes written down. As I read, I write down whatever I like. Some books offer me nothing to write down. Yours are rich with quotes, but they're longer than I can fit into that calendar. That's why there was only one quote.

While I'm thinking of it, Father V who came for mass today said that Dan Berigan, SJ (who was part of that civil disobedience during the Vietnam War) said, *"If you want to follow Christ, be sure you look good on wood."* Father V asked if we knew what that meant, adding that some priests he'd met didn't. We all knew it meant "the cross": If you want to follow Christ, make sure you look good on wood, because you will wear the cross. I thought that was powerful.

On following Christ

That cross remark relates to your taking a book rejection so positively. You're right, you know: There *is* something else on the horizon: A bigger publisher or whatever.

On releasing all things to God

It seems so many of us are at work bringing our visions to pass. This relates to our exchanges about releasing things to God in faith. I keep telling Sister M: *"If something is of God, it will work out."* I'm sure that's so with your publishing efforts.

I remember reading *Virtue of Trust* by Paul deJaegher, a long time ago. He's so right. Yesterday we had Scripture sharing with our new postulate (who is doing well). Some others were assembled with us, and the subject revolved around the idea of holiness and call. I said that everyone is called to contemplation. (I've said that to you a million times.) Then we considered the sentiments of those who quote Jesus' saying, *"I have chosen you."* My sense is that the call is there to everyone. Those with listening ears (or a listening heart) respond favorably; then God chooses. Of course, I'm not sure about that, but it does seem some people choose more actively to go forward. They never say "holiness is not for us." Holiness is for all, just as deJaegher wrote.

Holiness is for all

Even people who rob or are on drugs or alcohol are searching, too. Francis Thompson, the now-deceased poet who

All are called to holiness

117

wrote *The Hound of Heaven*, was a drug addict. Yet his poem is just beautiful. It uses the metaphor of God as the Hound: He chases us down in different ways. Although we say, "I sought You in this and I sought You in that," the Hound of Heaven is ever on our trail. Now there was a man who, despite being on drugs, contributed the most beautiful of poems. When I first entered the Sisters of Charity, that poem partly led me: The idea that we're all looking for God and looking in the wrong places, and that He's the Hound of Heaven, actively chasing after us and won't let us go. And so the poem is really for us, really a reminder.

It's never too late

The story in the gospel also highlights this: Remember the one about the vineyard owner who hires various laborers for his vineyard and when it's time for their pay, everyone receives the same amount. The ones who were hired first complain, "We worked longer." And the vineyard owner replies, "Are you jealous that I am generous?" So I agree it's never too late for us to receive our holiness.

Holiness is jelly beans

"*Just what is holiness?*" I asked when we shared Scripture yesterday. In our religious life we link that word with perfection — doing everything perfectly — but that's not it. The others teased me when I said, "Holiness is jelly beans." In other words, a jelly bean is being just a jelly bean, being and doing what it is *supposed* to be being and doing. (I'll have to ponder that some more.) Jesus says, "*Be ye perfect as your holy heavenly Father is perfect*," but before that he speaks compassionately about letting the rain fall on the good and the bad alike. That's how we should be. Perfect like that. Well, I won't get into religious gab here. I want to address your letter.

I had to laugh that you shut down the computer and had to get out storm candles. Very good that you had those. Attached to my outlet is a little electric candle with a timer that someone gave me for my birthday a couple years ago. Finally, this morning its light went on, just bright enough to wake me up. It's cute but wouldn't do in a big storm because it's electric.

On beauty and behavior

Isn't it nice you slept in until 7:00 a.m.? That's sweet. (Oh, I now read how much mail you get. How do you sort through all that?) Then I read that when you went out for

January

supplies, you found those trees down. The tree-trimmers may know you're the author who lives near them. Although as you say, little peppery women can agitate nearly anyone. (I'd call myself a little peppery woman, too.) Also, it's so dear the way you took out the tea in pretty bone-china cups and set it all out with the buzz saws and tractor. John Keats is right: *"A thing of beauty is a joy forever."* That everyone's comportment improved given the beauty of the cups, the flowering vines and your wind chimes is truly wonderful. What beauty can do.

And here, to keep you through the New Year, yet one more thought of St. Clare:

The Son of God himself made himself our way.

In peace,

MF.

...and while they are yet speaking,

I will hear. —Isaiah 65:24

EDITORS' AFTERWORD
Conversations at the Vital Ground of Being

After compiling these letters, we asked the two friends for their impressions of the final project. Rereading the letters, H said that MF seemed like the sister she never had, adding, "I wish everyone could be blessed with a spiritual friendship. It reflects an eternal unfolding, a conversation happening at the ground of vital Being—God Who meets me in the guise of this sister or that brother." Sister MF noted, "I feel like now my life will somehow go on, after I die, in this fine piece of work — this conversation with my other self."

All true friendship draws us into an intimacy of conversation, a word that means in part *tropos*: "a turning, a manner ... translated simply as 'be ye.'"[51] At best, discussions with our closest friends (even along secular themes) turn us toward them in love: We meet our friends halfway in the dialogue or exchange our thinking empathetically for their point of view.

A spiritual conversation is much more: Now we'd define it as *strepho*... a turning or *conversion* of mind toward the Divine[52] and a shift of mind and heart to God and away from human idols and attachments. The keynote of such exchange is transformative renewal of mind; it graces daily living. In a spiritual friendship not persons per se, but Love helps us accept our new name — Friend of God (much as occurred with our forefather Abraham).[53]

That turning phenomenon comes supernaturally and, as W.B. Vine emphasizes, the human agency is the responding *effect* of a holy grace, and Matthew 18: 23 also reveals:

And Jesus called a little child unto him and sat him in the midst of them, And said, Verily I say unto you, Except ye be converted and become as little children, ye shall not enter the kingdom of heaven.[54]

The actual Presence of God flows through the thoughts of a spiritual friendship, for one "whom God hath sent speaketh the words of God" (Jn 3: 34). That is the sacred, largely interior, conversation that God hears "while they are yet speaking."

Specifically, as these themes relate to the two friends, MF reports that her Community is building a new Monastery of St. Clare. H continues to scout for an aesthetic spot on which to build a hermitage. She writes daily and has just sold another manuscript. As of this book's publication, their spiritual dialogue progresses. They have yet to meet, in person.

The *Teleios* Editors

NOTES

1. Thomas Merton, Contemplative Prayer, New York: Image Books, 1990, p. 92 (italics for emphasis).
2. Abhishiktananda, Prayer, ISPCK, 1993 ed., transl. from French, Delhi, 110006, p. 29.
3. Thomas Merton, Contemplative Prayer, New York: Image Books, 1990, p. 54.
4. See Deut. 4: 21-24.
5. St. Clare from Heribert Roggen, The Spirit of St. Clare, Chicago, IL: Franciscan Herald Press, 1971.
6. Ibid.
(For more information about St. Clare, her devoted spiritual friendship with St. Francis of Assisi or the Order of St. Clare, please contact: Franciscan Herald Press, 1434 West 51st Street, Chicago, Illinois 60609.)
7. For a discussion about this see, for example, Marsha Sinetar, Ordinary People As Monks and Mystics, Mahwah, NJ: Paulist Press, 1986.
8. Meister Eckhart, Classics of Western Spirituality (German Works), Mahwah, NJ: Paulist Press, 1961 p. 183.
9. Evelyn Underhill, Mysticism, New York: E. P. Dutton, 1961, pp. 243; 442.
10. Jill Haak Adels, The Wisdom of the Saints (An Anthology), New York: Oxford University Press, 1987.
11. St. Francis of Assis, Writings and Early Biographies, Marion A. Habig, editor, Chicago Illinois: Franciscan Herald Press, (no date provided), p. 731-2.
12. Job 28: 17.
13. Marsha Sinetar, Ordinary People As Monks & Mystics, Mahwah, New Jersey: Paulist Press, 1986, p. 110.

Notes

14. Isaiah 65: 18-25.
15. John Hargreaves books and tapes available from Mulberry Press (POB 461) Carmel, California.
16. Paraphrased from Sister Benedicta, SLG, The Wisdom of the Desert Fathers, Oxford: SLG Press, 1975, p. 35.
17. Oswald Chambers, My Utmost for His Highest, Grand Rapids, MI: Barbour and Co., Inc., Discovery House Publishers, 1963 ed, p. 238.
18. Andrew Murray, The Ministry of Intercession, Kensington, PA: Whitaker House, 1982.
    _____, Prayer's Inner Chamber, London, UK: Pickering & Inglis, Ltd., 1989.
19. Oswald Chambers, My Utmost for His Highest, Grand Rapids, MI: Barbour and Co., Inc., Discovery House Publishers, 1963 ed.
20. Abraham Maslow, The Farther Reaches of Human Nature, New York: Viking Press, 1971, p. 208-209.
21. Ibid.
22. Evelyn Underhill, Mysticism, New York: E. P. Dutton, 1961, p. 215.
23. Ibid.
24. Meister Eckhart, The Essential Sermons, Commentaries, Treatises and Defense, trans. by E. Colledge and B. McGinn, New York: Paulist Press, 1961, p. 185.
25. Col. 2: 9-10.
26. John Beevers, Storm of Glory, New York: Image Books/Doubleday, 1949.
27. e.e. cummings, 100 Selected Poems, New York: Grove Press Edition, 1959, p. 96.
28. Bulletin of Monastic Interreligious Dialogue, Abbey of Gethsemani, 3642 Monks Road, Trappist, KY 40051-6102.
29. Evelyn Underhill, Mysticism, New York: E. P. Dutton, 1961.
30. Abhishiktananda, Prayer, I.S.P.C.K., 1993 ed., transl. from French, Delhi, 110006.
31. Jill Haak Adels, The Wisdom of the Saints (An Anthology), New York: Oxford University Press, 1987.
32. Jean Leclerq, Bernard of Clairvaux, Kalamazoo, MI: Cistercian Publications, 1976, p. 161.
33. John Beevers, Storm of Glory, New York: Image Books/Doubleday, 1949.
34. Oswald Chambers, My Utmost for His Highest, Grand Rapids, MI: Barbour and Co., Inc., Discovery House, 1963 ed., p. 67.
35. Ibid, p. 195.
36. II Cor. 15: 54.
37. Laurie Lisle, Portrait of an Artist, New York: Washington Square Press, 1981, p. 347.

Notes

38. Thomas Merton, The Monastic Journey, New York: Image Books/Doubleday, 1978, p. 88.
39. Luke 10: 38-42.
40. Julian of Norwich, Revelations of Divine Love, New York: Penguin Books, 1966.
41. Andrew Murray, The Ministry of Intercession, Kensington, PA: Whitaker House, 1982, p. 84.
42. Jean Leclerq, Bernard of Clairvaux, Kalamazoo, MI: Cistercian Publications, 1976, p. 161.
43. Marsha Sinctar, The Mentor's Spirit, 1995; work in progress.
44. Andrew Murray, The Ministry of Intercession, Kensington, PA: Whitaker House, 1982.
45. Proverb 11: 24-5.
46. Lawrence S. Cunningham, "Praying the Psalms: some notes," America, August 1, 1997, p. 8.
47. Ibid, p. 10.
48. Evelyn Underhill, Mysticism, New York: E. P. Dutton, 1961, p. 423.
49. E. Allison Peers trans. and editor, Interior Castle by St. Teresa of Avila, New York: Image Books, 1961.
50. Paul deJaegher, S.J., The Virtue of Trust, New York: P. J. Kennedy & Sons, 1931.
51. In W. B. Vine, An Expository Dictionary of New Testament Words, Nashville, TN: Thomas Nelson, (no date provided), p. 230-231.
52. Ibid.
53. James 2: 23.
54. Matthew 18: 23.

BIBLIOGRAPHY

Abhishiktananda, *Prayer*, I.S.P.C.K, 1993 ed., trans. from French, Delhi, 110006.

Jill Haak Adels, *The Wisdom of the Saints* (An Anthology), New York: Oxford University Press, 1987.

John Beevers, *Storm of Glory*, New York: Image Books/Doubleday, 1949.

Sister Benedicta, SLG, *The Wisdom of the Desert Fathers*, Oxford: SLG Press, 1975.

John Beevers, *Storm of Glory*, New York: Image Books/Doubleday, 1949.

Bulletin of Monastic Interreligious Dialogue, Abbey of Gethsemani, 3642 Monks Road, Trappist, KY 40051-6102.

Oswald Chambers, *My Utmost for His Highest*, Grand Rapids, MI: Barbour and Co., Inc., Discovery House Publishers, 1963 ed.

Col. 2: 9-10.

II Cor. 15:54.

e.e. cummings, *100 Selected Poems*, New York: Grove Press Edition, 1959.

Lawrence S. Cunningham, "Praying the Psalms: some notes," *America*, August 1, 1997.

Paul deJaegher, S.J., *The Virtue of Trust*, New York: P. J. Kennedy & Sons, 1931.

Deut. 4: 21-24.

R. M. French, editor, *The Way of the Pilgrim*, New York: Seabury, 1965.

Marion A. Habig, editor, *St. Francis of Assis, Writings and Early Biographies*, Chicago, IL: Franciscan Herald Press (No date provided).

Bibliography

John Hargreaves books and tapes available from Mulberry Press (POB 461) Carmel, California.

Isaiah 65: 18-25.

James 2: 23.

Job 28: 17.

Julian of Norwich, *Revelations of Divine Love*, New York: Penguin Books, 1966.

Jean Leclerq, *Bernard of Clairvaux*, Kalamazoo, MI: Cistercian Publications, 1976.

Laurie Lisle, *Portrait of an Artist*, New York: Washington Square Press, 1981.

Luke 10: 38-42.

Abraham Maslow, *The Farther Reaches of Human Nature*, New York: Viking Press, 1971.

Matthew 18: 23.

Meister Eckhart, Classics of Western Spirituality (German Works), Mahwah, NJ: Paulist Press, 1961.

Thomas Merton, *Contemplative Prayer*, New York: Image Books, 1990.

Thomas Merton, *The Monastic Journey*, New York: Image Books/Doubleday, 1978.

Andrew Murray, *The Ministry of Intercession*, Kensington, PA: Whitaker House, 1982.

Andrew Murray, *Prayer's Inner Chamber*, London, UK: Pickering & Inglis, Ltd., 1989.

E. Allison Peers trans. and editor, *Interior Castle by St. Teresa of Avila*, New York: Image Books, 1961.

Prov. 11: 24-5.

St. Clare from Heribert Roggen, *The Spirit of St. Clare*, Chicago, IL: Franciscan Herald Press, 1971.

Marsha Sinetar, *The Mentor's Spirit*, 1995; work in progress.

_____, *Ordinary People As Monks and Mystics*, Mahwah, NJ: Paulist Press, 1986.

Jean Sulivan, *Morning Light*, Mahwah, NJ: Paulist Press, 1988.

Evelyn Underhill, *Mysticism*, New York: E. P. Dutton, 1961.

W. B. Vine, *An Expository Dictionary of New Testament Words*, Nashville, TN: Thomas Nelson, (no date provided).

ABBREVIATED SUBJECT INDEX, BY MONTH

A	attachments, breaking of:	Jan	I	impoverished new church	May/Jun
	assertion	Aug		inward listening	July
B	Beauty, as healer	Jan	J	jelly beans as holy	July
	Beauty & Behavior	Jan	L	letting go as love	Jan
C	contemplative life	Jan		Lord's care of us	Oct
	completion, per Julian of N	July/Aug		leadings, God's	Oct
	completion & commitment	Aug	M	Martha vs Mary	Nov
	Community, questions of	Sept		mirror literature	Jan
	courage, discussion of	Oct		Mary, leadings of	Aug
D	death, worshipful	Nov		Mary, Perfect Mother	July
	Divine Synchrony	Feb		Mind of Christ	Aug
	delays, dealing with	Mar/Apr		monks, what they do	Oct
	doubts, Julian's handling of	Nov		mystics in childhood	Oct
	discernment, cloistered life	Dec	N	never too late	Jan
	divisions, none in heaven	Aug	O	optimism of saints	Jan
E	Eucharist, described	Oct	P	prayers	Jan
	Everything leads to God	Oct		paradox, spiritual	Nov
	Encouragement, spiritual	Jan	R	rejection & faith	Dec/Jan
F	Faith, leaps of	Nov		rejection & growth	Nov
	faith, developing via trials	Nov	S	"seekers," defined	Aug
	foundation stone	Feb		self-forgetting	Aug
	Franciscan peace	May/June		sleep & prayer	Sept
	formal vs informal spirit	Aug		saints, trust of	Oct
	forgiveness, pre-existing	Sept		spiritual friendship	Oct/Nov
	forgiveness & Julian of N	Sept	T	thoughts, God's	Feb
	Following Christ	Jan		true friends	Mar/Apr
G	genuine interest of others	Jan		true contemplatives	Aug
	giving, truest form of	Jan		trust of God	Dec
	grace & blessings	Aug		time, use of at night	Dec
H	Holy Spirit as energy	Jan	V	Victor of Life, poem	Aug
	hiddenness	Feb	W	weaker ones, love of	Aug
	honoring parents	Mar/Apr		Wheat & Tares, parable	

129